Praise for *Teaching the Invisible Race*

"DelaRosa's book, *Teaching the Invisible Race*, offers genuine ways for Asian Americans to be seen and heard. DelaRosa puts the teachings of our ancestors in conversation with current and future educators by weaving together spoken word, stories, historical evidence, and what I believe is most compelling—pauses in the text—where we ask ourselves questions about what we are learning and what it does to us. It is here, where we ALL become visible.

Dr. Allyson Tintiangco-Cubales, professor of Ethnic Studies, San Francisco State University

"What do you remember being taught about Asian American History in your K-12 education experience? What Asian American scholars and heroes can you name without looking them up? With *Teaching the Invisible Race*, Tony DelaRosa fills in a crucial gap in scholarship for educators and he does so in a book that is engaging, practical, and inspiring. Thank you, Tony, for bringing this important work to the field."

Dr. Tina Owen-Moore, superintendent at School District of Cudahy, Wisconsin

"Tony DelaRosa is the champion we all need. As a fellow parent and journalist, it is so exciting to see Tony taking these tremendous steps to make meaningful change in the lives of our children! We need to celebrate all of our contributions, including that of our very large, diverse, and complex Asian diaspora."

Michelle Li, founder of Very Asian Foundation & Reporter

"Tony DelaRosa is a voice of a generation. His bravery and expertise makes him a voice we all must take note and learn from. In the face of censorship, *Teaching the Invisible Race* is an urgent read and resource for anyone who cares about the fate of future generations."

Tonya Mosley, journalist, cohost of NPR's "Fresh Air"

Teaching the Invisible Race

Teaching the Invisible Race

Embodying a Pro-Asian American Lens in Schools

Tony DelaRosa

JB JOSSEY-BASS™
A Wiley Brand

Published by John Wiley & Sons, Inc., Hoboken, New Jersey.
Published simultaneously in Canada.

For general information on our other products and services or for technical support, please contact our Customer Care Department within the United States at (800) 762-2974, outside the United States at (317) 572-3993 or fax (317) 572-4002.

Wiley also publishes its books in a variety of electronic formats. Some content that appears in print may not be available in electronic formats. For more information about Wiley products, visit our web site at www.wiley.com.

Library of Congress Control Number:

Hardback: 9781119930235
ePDF: 9781119930259
epub: 9781119930242

Cover Design: Wiley

SKY10054881_090723

To. . .

My son, Sebastian Rizal DelaRosa.

My Pampangan & Caviteño Ancestors: Apung Dena, Grandma Clarita, and Grandpa Tony.

My Filipinx/a/o American Artists, Educators, Community-Engaged Scholars, and Activists.

The Asian American Avengers of past and present, both in and out of this book.

Contents

Foreword

During one of my early years as a classroom teacher, I was patting myself on the back for completing a unit on the social construction of race with my third grade class. I asked my students to journal about their experience throughout the lessons and to write down their reflections and any lingering questions. As I flipped through their responses and congratulated myself, I came across a question from a student that knocked me off my pedestal: "Why haven't we talked about my race?"

What floored me was that this honest question was written by one of my Asian students. How could I, an Asian American, a self-proclaimed social justice educator, have made such an egregious mistake?

I spent the following hours, days, and weeks racking my memory of my own experiences as a K–12 student. When did my teachers bring up Asian American history? When had I ever been invited to explore my identity as an adopted, Jewish, Korean American girl?

The unfortunate truth was, there wasn't much to reflect upon. In elementary school, Asian celebrations were often lumped into lessons such as "holidays around the world." There was minimal representation in our picture books, like *The Korean Cinderella* and *Tikki Tikki Tembo*, both written by white authors and spoiler—the books haven't aged well. In middle school, we read *The Good Earth* by Pearl S. Buck (also a white woman). When high school rolled around, we barely touched on Chinese laborers who built the railroads, and anything we learned about the Vietnam War was presented from the American perspective.

Looking back, I realize I was perpetuating the same erasure I had experienced as a student. Since I had no model or exemplar of what culturally responsive, anti-bias Asian American education could look like, I had difficulty bringing it to life in my own practice. There was a staggering amount of learning and unlearning I needed to do.

Tony and I formed our friendship through social media, sharing ideas, and supporting each other's work. The first time we met in person was at a Teach for America's Asian American and Pacific Islander gathering in 2020, about three weeks before the world shut down. We ate dim sum, drank boba, and called ourselves "The Asian Avengers." None of us knew how lucky we would be to come together at this time, how we would lean on one another in the months and years to come, and how our professional relationships and friendships would only grow stronger with time.

Tony's debut, *Teaching the Invisible Race*, could not have come at a better time as it is relevant in a multitude of spaces. It is truly the book that I not only wish I had read when I began my path as an educator, but also the book I wish had been available for my own teachers to learn from. I'm grateful to call Tony a friend, peer, and teacher.

Teaching the Invisible Race is unlike any book you're likely to come across on the subject of Asian American education. Tony blends his unique skills as a classroom teacher, mentor, poet, researcher, and activist to connect the personal with the intellectual. He shares his stunning lyrical voice with his audience, while also providing historical context, academic frameworks, and practical examples of how this work can come to life in the classroom.

I am so grateful to you, Dear Reader, for picking up this book so we can come together and not only represent but also affirm the histories and identities of the Asian American community.

In solidarity,

Liz Kleinrock

founder, Teach and Transform

author, *Start Here Start Now: A Guide to Anti-bias and Anti-racist Work in Your School Community*

How Will They Hold Us?

On May 31, 2021, HB 376, also known as the TEAACH Act, passed in Illinois, mandating that Asian American history be taught across the state. The TEAACH Act spurred other states to follow suit. The following poem was also published previously in the *Asian American Policy Review* at the Harvard Kennedy School and featured in the Hulu special "Heritage Heroes."

What separates a mandate from a movement
are the shepherds who inherit the stories.
And what will teachers do with us?
"Fastest growing racial group"
48 countries deep
2300+ languages
and an ocean of dialects
Who will carry our stories?
Will they cradle us precious
like Yuri did Malcolm
at his darkest of hours?
Like the Black Panthers did Yellow and Brown Power
Like at the International Hotel, Philippine
American War,
Or like Blasian March building Black, Asian, and
Blasian radical rapport?

How loud will they teach this "invisible race"
Beyond the silence outside of October and May?
What if they drop one of us?
Will they pick us up like a fallen soldier
or will they stumble over a minefield
and fumble us forgotten?
Who entrusted them
with our spices, jackfruit, and diamonds?
Will they style us windows and pick up a mirror?

*Will they dance a revolution or will they wallflower
reform?*
*Will they wade in the binary or swim ultraviolet
and upstream?*
Will they study our mountains and movements?
   Do they know us beyond a hashtag?
   Beyond San Francisco and Time Square?
   *beyond the Black & white binary that flattens
   and binds us?*
Can they name our mothers before our fathers?
Can they even name our fathers?
Will they name themselves now: "allies"
After they discover our names in a book club
that doesn't scent of our vinegar, sweat,
blood, and dust?
When the time comes, will they play our battle drums?
Or will they steal or plant our Chrysanthemums?

About the Author

Tony DelaRosa (he/siya) is an award winning Filipino American anti-bias and anti-racist educator, leadership coach, motivational speaker, spoken word poet, racial equity strategist, and researcher. He holds a BA in Asian Studies at the University of Cincinnati, a M.Ed with a focus on Arts Education and Non-Profit Management at Harvard University, and is currently pursuing his PhD in Education Leadership and Policy Analysis at the University of Wisconsin Madison as an Education Graduate Research Scholar. In 2021, he received the INSPIRE Award given by the National Association of Asian American Professionals and United Airlines. In 2023, he received the Community Trailblazer Award from The Asian American Foundation (TAAF), where his work is featured on TAAF's Heritage Heroes documentary streaming on Hulu.

His work has also been featured in NPR, *Harvard Ed Magazine*, the Smithsonian, Columbia University's Hechinger Report, *Hyphen Magazine*: Asian American Unabridged, and elsewhere. He has co-founded NYC's first Asian American teacher support, development, and retention initiative called AATEND under NYC Men Teach, the NYC DOE, and Office of the Mayor. He served as a director of Leadership Development at Teach for America coaching teachers and leading DEI strategy. Today, he coaches CEOs and principals on crafting and refining their short-term and long-term DEI strategy.

In his free time he enjoys spending time with his wife and son and checking out the latest hit RPG or anime series.

Follow him on IG and Twitter at @TonyRosaSpeaks.

Acknowledgments

I wrote this book on Tequesta (Miami, FL) and HoChunk (Madison, WI) land. It's important to first acknowledge them as original inheritors and nurturers of these regions to remind ourselves that we are guests and settlers on someone else's land. The land acknowledgment is a way of grounding you in decolonial thought as you approach this book.

This is a perfect segue into my second acknowledgment, which is to highlight my Filipino ancestors. While the Filipinos were the first Asian settlers in the United States in 1587, we don't learn about them in school. So allow me to shout out a few Filipino revolutionaries: Larry Itliong, Al Robles, Philip Vera Cruz, Gabriela Silong, Carlos Bulosan, Dr. Jose Rizal, and Dr. Dawn Mabalon. Being unapologetically Filipino and Filipino American and taking up space gave me the confidence, wisdom, and makibaka ("fight" in Tagalog) to speak truth to power through poetry, education, and critical analysis. Because of you all, I'm helping shape the education sector and co-define, amongst other Filipino American critical scholars, what it means to have a Filipino American critical ethnic lens on the world.

Third, I have to thank my "Asian American Avengers" both in and out of this book. I first heard of this term when I was consulting with the Smithsonian Asian Pacific American Center with a group of Asian American educators, scholars, and activists. I'm applying this term to any Asian American activist in their respective fields. The first few people I will thank are: Cap Aguilar, Sarah Ha, and Soukprida Phetmisy. These three Asian American women lifted me up during my education practitioner years. Cap and I worked together in Boston where she amplified my story and cultivated healing, reflective, and celebratory spaces for Asian American teachers on top of doing her job as a coach to 40 teachers during that time. Sarah Ha invited me to share my spoken word poem at a large affinity space at the Teach for America 25th Anniversary Summit and guided me as I led my first Asian American, Native Hawaiian, and Pacific Islander (AANHPI) teacher leadership summit in Oakland, CA. Soukprida Phetmisy and I co-led the AANHPI teacher leadership summit. Since then, Soukprida and I have supported each other's endeavors through art, activism, and storytelling. We hold each other close.

Fourth, I'm amplifying my mentors at the Harvard Graduate School of Education (HGSE) who I met in 2018, and stay connected to through my work. I have to start off with Dr. Tracie Jones who was the former director of Diversity, Equity, and Inclusion at HGSE and now an assistant dean at MIT. She took me in and believed that an Asian American could and should lead Harvard's largest education conference for people of color called the "Alumni of Color Conference," or AOCC. She trained me to be a cross-racial coalition advocate, an entrepreneur, and community builder.

This book would also not be true without the mentorship of Dr. Christina Villarreal (Dr. V), my ethnic studies professor. Ethnic studies changed my life. You'll hear that from many students of ethnic studies because ethnic studies is a way of life. Dr. V's super-power is designing and leading critical discussions, while holding everyone in her spaces with love and compassion. Her classroom is the definition of abolitionist teaching because it bridges the class with community and inspires radical thought and stretches our imaginations. This leads me to Dr. Josephine Kim (Dr. Jo). She was my advisor when I co-led the Pan-Asian Coalition for Education (PACE). She guided me in centering Asian American studies and narratives at HGSE. Later, I got to serve as a teaching fellow for the inaugural Asian American studies course that she designed: H503M Race, Ethnicity, and Culture: Contemporary Issues in Asian America. In teaching and leading in H503M, I realized that one of my life's purposes is to amplify Asian American education through a critical ethnoracial lens everywhere I go. This class pushed me to pursue my doctorate.

Beyond the communities I've been directly involved in, I have to thank everyone who continues to support my own development as a community-engaged scholar in ethnic studies: Ron Rapatalo, Richard Haynes, Jermona Intia, Amnat Chittaphong, Andrea Kim, The Board, Patrick Armstrong, Richard Leong, Dr. Kiona, Kim Saira, Dr. Christopher Emdin, Dr. Yolanda Sealey-Ruiz, Dr. Judy Yu, Dr. Travis Bristol, Jerry Won, Liz Kleinrock, NAAAP, Francesca Hong, Kabby Hong, Michelle Li, the EdGRS Fellowship at UW-Madison, Dr. Anjalé Welton, Dr. Erica Turner, Dr. Lesley Bartlett, Dr. Kevin Lawrence Henry, Dr. Karen Buenavista Hanna, Dr. Liza Talusan, Dr. E. J. David Ramos, and of course the beloved Dr. Kevin Nadal. Shout out to my fellow authors, Liz Kleinrock, Bianca Mabute-Louie, and Kwame Sarfo-Mensah, for holding space for me to exchange ideas about the book (excited to be in the lab with you).

Big thanks to my acquisitions editor, Amy Fandrei, who saw me talk with Elena Aguilar on an Instagram Live Chat about coaching practices, and believed I had a story to tell. Thank you Jossey-Bass team for investing in me and the Asian American community through the development of this book.

Salamat to Ruby and Willy Delarosa (aka Mom and Dad). Your support since day one cannot be measured. From cradle to critical consciousness, you have pushed me to learn so much about who I am today and how I see the world.

Salamat to Ateh Roo (Rubilly DelaRosa aka my sis). You cheered me on from the start. You introduced me to poetry, and that opened up a portal to radical imagination. Thank you for the wonderful doodles you drew of the Asian American Avengers; your art is your activism.

Lastly, thank you to my wife and son. My son, Sebastian Rizal DelaRosa, lit a fire in me around why this work matters personally. I always had a passion for social justice, but now it feels so much more proximate that you are in our lives and heading to school. My wife and best friend, Stephanie Jimenez, showered me with love and support through reading, editing, and pushing my ideas to the fore. I would not be the feminist I am today without you.

Introduction

Dear Reader, thank you for holding this book. The way we hold each other is what grounds me in critical hope in times of crisis and in times of joy. It's 2023, and the Asian American community is facing a rising crisis of hate, racism, and violence stemming from systems of colonialism, exploitation, racial capitalism, xenophobia, sinophobia, white supremacy, and anti-blackness.

Asian Americans know that this has been happening to us long before the pandemic. In the United States, anti-Asian sentiment stems from racist and exclusionist policies like the 1790 Naturalization Act that restricted naturalization to only people identifying as "white." Anti-Asian sentiment stems from the 1882 Chinese Exclusion Act, which for decades banned Chinese people from entering the United States. This act was extended to people from the Philippines, India, and Japan (indeed, an entire "barred Asiatic zone" was established in 1917), lumping different national-origin groups into a single racial category, the "Asiatic" (Ngai, 2021). Anti-Asian sentiment is an American tradition set forth by some of our nation's leaders:

◆ President Franklin D. Roosevelt with Executive Order 9066 (the internment of Japanese Americans)

◆ President Lyndon B. Johnson's Hart-Cellar Act of 1965 (shifting an immigrant quota system to a merit-based system)

◆ President Donald J. Trump's Executive Order 13769 in 2017 (also known as the "Muslim Ban")

Today the number of anti-Asian hate and violence incidents is reportedly soaring above 11,000, according to the organization Stop AAPI Hate 2022 report, which collected data between March 19, 2020, and March 31, 2022. These statistics don't even consider unreported incidents. Holding this book means you see us, hear us, and empathize with us.

The poem you read on the previous pages emerged from witnessing a wave of Asian American education policy slowly taking root across the United States. Of course I have to pay homage to the 1960's ethnic studies movement that manifested because of the Third World Liberation Front. While ethnic studies is mostly a bicoastal movement, specific Asian American students K–12 mandates began occurring recently, starting in Illinois with the Teach Equitable Asian American Community History Act (TEAACH Act). After the Act passed, many coalitions followed suit in different states, such as the Make Us Visible Connecticut and Make Us Visible New Jersey.

I chose the title *Teaching the Invisible Race*, because despite the anti–Asian American policies and incidents that I have outlined at large, people still render us *invisible* through gaslighting our oppression, excluding us from social justice education and conversations, through intentional omission, and homogenizing our vast and diverse experiences.

While my poem at the beginning of the book critiques how teachers as "shepherds" will hold us (teach our stories), this book aims at helping educators understand how to strengthen their own Asian American ethno-racial literacy in order to teach it to their students. The outcome is culturally responsive and sustaining, paying homage to Dr. Gloria Ladson-Billings's evolved work in Culturally Responsive-Sustaining Pedagogy. *Teaching the Invisible Race* is Halo Halo, "mix-mix" in Tagalog. When I say Halo Halo, I mean this book is a remix of story, poetry, concepts, theory, framework, case studies, interviews, and more. Beyond the fight of combating anti-Asian sentiment, violence, and racism within ourselves and within the communities we serve, I'm pushing educators to hold both our fight and our joy together. To hold us close means you hold us beyond this moment and through this next stage of an evergreen movement.

The Term "Pro–Asian American"

CUNY professor Kevin Nadal explains how the terms "Yellow Power" and "Brown Power" stem from the Black Power Movement in the 1960s-70s. In a similar light, I'm using the contemporary term "pro–Asian American" as an inspiration from the Black community who founded the term "pro-Black" as a response to Black dehumanization and celebration for Black identity, history, culture, power, and futures.

In searching for the origins of the concept of "pro-Black," scholar mentors and friends pointed me to Marcus Garvey, a Black nationalist and pan-Africanist, who founded the Universal Negro Improvement Association (UNIA) in the 1920s, which stressed Black pride, racial unity of African Americans, and a need to redeem Africa from white rule (Hill, 1983). Others have pointed me to the "Black is Beautiful" movement founded by Kwame Brathwaite and Elombe Brath in the 1960s-70s, which broadly focused on embracing Black culture and identity, with a sub-focus on emotional and psychological well-being (National Museum of African American History & Culture). In a similar light, this book aims at exploring and educating on what it means to be pro–Asian American.

Asian American people have acted pro–Asian American without even labeling their actions as such through the building of Asian American employee resource groups, affinity spaces, businesses, movies, networks, and more. In a similar ethos to pro-Blackness, "pro–Asian American" balances the concept of combating or fighting anti-Asian hate and racism, since it is a symptom of white supremacy. "Pro–Asian American" means you are actively supporting the Asian American community with a big focus on low-income Asian American communities that go invisible due to the model minority myth (i.e., Hmong, Lao, Chinese, Filipino, Vietnamese, Thai, Cambodian, and more). "Pro–Asian American" means you are actively supporting Asian Americans with the notion that our liberation is tied to combating anti-Blackness and embodying a pro-Black lens. We owe our freedom to radical Black activists and organizers, many of whom are queer, trans, and non-binary, who paved the path for us to thrive as a community. I speak more about the history of Black-and-Asian American relations later in the book when talking about Isang Bagsak pedagogy and cross-racial solidarity.

Who Does This Book Center?

This book centers the narratives of Asian Americans: East, South, and Southeast. For clarity, East Asian refers to: mainland China,

South Korea, North Korea, Japan, Hong Kong, Taiwan, and Macau. South Asia refers to Bangladesh, Bhutan, India, Maldives, Nepal, Pakistan, and Sri Lanka with Afghanistan also often included. Southeast Asia refers to the Philippines, Indonesia, Laos, Vietnam, Cambodia, Malaysia, Brunei, East Timor (or Timor-Leste), Myanmar, Singapore, and Thailand. This book does not center West Asian Americans, Central Asian Americans, Native Hawaiians, and Pacific Islanders because they deserve their own books, and this book will not do these communities justice as it pertains to education. This is not to say that I won't mention narratives or histories from these areas, because I know there are many overlaps around cross-racial coalitions in the fight for labor rights, in the fight against colonization, and in the fight for visibility in education. There is also overlap when we think about Asian Pacific Islander American Heritage Month (APIHM) in May.

Who Is the Audience?

Teaching the Invisible Race is geared toward upper elementary through high school English language arts, reading, social studies, and US history practitioners including teachers, instructional coaches, curriculum specialists, and anyone who has a stake in the realm of teaching and learning. This includes school administrators and counselors. This is the area of expertise that I taught and coached while working directly in schools. The examples and reproducibles in this book will reflect these content areas and grade levels. This book is also for those who identify as white, as well as who identify as People of Color (POC).

The Writing Process, Theories, Analysis, and Inquiry

While this is very much a practitioner's book, there are a few qualitative research logics that influenced my writing process, from the book design to the intake of interviews and readings and to the analysis of the content. These logics come from autoethnography, portraiture, narrative inquiry, community-engaged scholarship, and Asian Crit.

Autoethnography allowed me to share my own story as a Filipino American spoken word artist. Spoken word poetry is a dialectic, and like the best forms of pedagogy, dialogue with self, student, and community is paramount. With the reflection questions placed throughout the book, they ask you to stop and reflect. This methodology influenced the beginning cadence of every chapter with the section entitled "The Personal Is Political." I also wanted to emphasize the messiness that is being a Filipino American poet who has lived in San Diego, California, Cincinnati, Ohio, Indianapolis, Indiana, Boston, Massachusetts, Miami, Florida and now Madison, Wisconsin. Each place and time period influences how I think and write about being Asian American in the United States, which makes for a narrative hyper-conscious of context.

Portraiture is the methodology that I learned from my former advisor at Harvard Graduate School of Education, Dr. Sara Lawrence-Lightfoot. Dr. Lawrence-Lightfoot pioneered this qualitative inquiry method in 1983 helping researchers understand the social, cultural, and political aspects of a place over time. Portraiture bridges art and science, examining the empirical with the aesthetic. You can see portraiture through myself having built a deep connection to the Asian American community to understand the social, cultural, and political aspects of our community both before, during, and after the #StopAsianHate movement. Being empirical about disaggregating the Asian American experience through a lens of intersectionality is necessary because it is living proof that we are more than a monolith.

The stereotype of Asian Americans is monochromatic, flattened and uninspiring, and I know that our community is the exact opposite. We are ultralight beams, buried in the past, and bursting into the future. Another aspect of portraiture is explicitly focusing on the "goodness" of the portrait and narrative around Asian Americans. When I refer to "goodness," this is not to be confused with "success" and the trap of the model minority myth, but rather helping us unpack what it means to be "pro–Asian American." Goodness, in the interpretive frame, means that the interviews are beautifully and compellingly written to celebrate self. How often do we get to see Asian American narratives celebrate themselves outside of the bento-boxed stereotypes that the United States media has restricted us in? Also, "goodness" refers to this concept of being able to transport the "goods" or "qualities" of Asian America to the reader.

I chose narrative inquiry and a community-engaged scholarship as approaches because it was the best mode to connect the dots between my autoethnography and the ethnography of Asian American artivists and education practitioners already embodying a pro–Asian American lens in their work. Similar to what Dr. Gloria Ladson-Billings in *The Dream Keepers* states about objectivity, while I accept the empirical information about Asian Americans, I want to underscore "the primacy of objectivity" to help all of us lean into the messiness that is the Asian American experience. Community-engaged scholarship, in particular, rooted my work with a power-with framework across the Asian American interviewees that hold differing intersectionalities than my own, which dovetails into Asian Crit.

Asian Crit (or Asian Critical Race Theory) grew out of critical race scholarship, which focused more on a Black and white binary of analyzing how race and racism are endemic to the United States. Scholars such as Mari Matsuda and Robert S. Chang are early pioneers of this work. From the early work in 2013 of Dr. Samuel D. Museus and Dr. Jon S. Iftikar, they break down the AsianCrit framework into seven tenets:

- ◆ *Asianization,* the notion that racism is pervasive in society and racializes Asian Americans in distinct ways.

- ◆ *Transnational contexts,* the importance of recognizing that the lives of Asian Americans are shaped by historical/contemporary national and transnational contexts.

- ◆ *(Re)Constructive History,* the necessity to (re)construct history to include the voices and experiences of Asian Americans.

- ◆ *Strategic (Anti)essentialism,* the idea that dominant forces impact the racialization of Asian Americans in society and the ways that they reify and/or disrupt this racialization of themselves and other People of Color.

- ◆ *Intersectionality,* the notion that racism and other systems of oppression intersect in multiple ways and in multiple spaces.

◆ *Story, theory, and praxis,* that counterstories constructed by Asian Americans, theory, and practice must inform one another and should all be used for transformative purposes.

◆ *Commitment to social justice,* that the utilization of AsianCrit is a means to ending all forms of oppression. All of these tenets are core theories that influence how I talk about my story, the story of Asian America, and the charge for practitioners to teach us with nuance and care.

While I don't explicitly name all of the tenets of Asian Crit throughout the book, you will see connections to these concepts throughout.

How This Book Is Structured

This book has four main parts that divide the chapters.

◆ Part 1: "Teach Us Visible by Seeing and Remembering Us"
◆ Part 2: "Teach Us Visible by Centering Us"
◆ Part 3: "Teach Us Visible by Celebrating Us"
◆ Part 4: "Teach Us Visible by Moving with Us"

Part 1, "Teach Us Visible by Seeing and Remembering Us," contains Chapters 1–4. Chapter 1, "What do you know about Asian America?" begins with a self-assessment on how much you know about Asian American history, narratives, and studies as a whole. This was inspired by Liz Kleinrock's assessment for her students regarding Asian American narratives. The assessment does not aim to give you a rating, but more closely to force you to consider how much or little you know about Asian American topics.

Chapter 2, "Windows, Mirrors, and Sliding Glass Doors Framework," focuses on Emily Styles and Rudine Sims Bishop's work. Outside of reflecting on "the amount of knowledge," this method will enable you to connect to the book from your ethnoracial positionality. If you are an Asian American, then this book might serve as a mirror, as well as a window to other Asian American narratives. I acknowledge that Asian America is highly complex and we are not monolithic, however some of our stories do overlap across the diaspora, such as our relationship to exclusion, the model minority myth, and our relationships within the binary of white supremacy and anti-Blackness. For non–Asian American people of color, this book might serve as both a mirror and window at times. As a white person, this book will serve as a window as you look into our histories, narratives, and pedagogies. At the end of Chapter 2, I charge you to create Sliding Glass Doors through the teaching of Asian American history and narratives.

Chapters 3 and 4 offer a timeline of laws, policies, and events that have had both a negative and positive impact in shaping the political landscape of Asian America today. Chapter 3, "Timeline of Anti–Asian American Racism and Violence," should act as a reference because Asian Americans are often gaslighted with comments or treatment that dismisses their relationship to racism in the United States. In Chapter 4, "Timeline of Pro–Asian American Milestones and Permissions," I offer a timeline of laws, policies, and events that symbolize Asian American milestones that have shaped the political power and landscape of Asian Americans. Understanding both positive and negative laws, policies, and events in history helps foster the knowledge base required to be pro–Asian American. After Part 1 of the book, which sets the tone and grounds us on how to navigate the book, the rest of the parts are less linear. Based on the self-assessment, I encourage you to visit portions of the book that help you fill in gaps in knowledge or strengthens concepts that need extra love.

Part 2 of this book entitled, "Teach Us Visible by Centering Us." The ethos behind centering us underscores the concepts of Asian American identity, intersectionality, and how we exist beyond the Black and white binary. This part of the book includes Chapters 5–10. Chapter 5 dives you into the intersectionality and plurality of Asian Americans. You often hear the slogan, "we are not a monolith" — because time and time again the media portrays us as such. It provides an activity called "Living Portraits" to ensure that Asian American perspectives are leveraged in class discussion 365 days per year.

Chapter 6, "Isang Bagsak as an Educational Framework," challenges the Black and white binary because it explores how practitioners can teach enmeshed histories. Chapter 6 also breaks the Filipino concept of "Isang Bagsak" into a pedagogical tool. Chapter 7, "Colonization, War, Colonial Mentality, and Settler

Colonialism," dives deeper into why colonialism is at the center of many of the issues we face, such as white supremacy, paternalism, racial capitalism, and more. Being able to know this and teach it will allow educators to make stronger connections to other countries and communities impacted by colonialism.

Chapter 8, "Asian American Queer and Trans Perspectives." This chapter includes queer and trans theory, information about Asian American queer and trans outcomes in schools, and interviews between two Asian American activist leaders, Soukprida Phetmisy and Paul Tran. I end this part of the book with Chapter 9 entitled "Immigration and Undocu–Asian American," which defines what it means to be Undocu-Asian. I invite Assistant Professor Dr. Rose Ann Gutierrez from the University of Nevada-Reno to tell her story and share her knowledge as an expert on this topic.

To finalize Part 2, I end with Chapter 10 entitled "Asian Americans, Disability Narratives, and Crip Ecology. This chapter includes voices from my auntie Arlene Fuertes, poet and educator Kay Ulanday Barrett, and disability justice activist Miso Kwak.

While Part 1 of this book helps build the container for shared language and Part 2 expands our perspectives regarding Asian America, Part 3 shifts toward strengthening your pro–Asian American lens through Art (Chapter 11) and Pop Culture (Chapter 12). I end the previous poem specifically with this line, "Will they play our battle drums? / Will they plant our Chrysanthemums?" to charge educators to fight for and with us while toasting to our accomplishments, joy, and mere existence. Chapter 11, "Teaching Us Visible Through Art, Poetry, and Hip-Hop," investigates the power of hip-hop, poetry, and visual arts. Educators rarely get the opportunity to activate the visual and artistic lens that our students' possess, and this chapter holds space for that. Chapter 12, "Teaching Asian American Studies Through Pop Culture," points us to the present. Much of what shapes the public's racial literacy of Asian America comes from popular culture. In this chapter, I highlight a few personal moments that have shaped my knowledge of Asian America, and invite DEI strategist from Collective, Richard Leong, to tell his story and share his expertise through Asian American pop culture education.

After exploring Asian American art and pop culture, we move to Part 4, "Teach Us Visible by Moving with Us." This is the final section of the book which focuses on the present and future.

Chapter 13, "Working with Asian American Students, Staff, and Families," refocuses our lens on the very people we aim to support through building our pro–Asian American lens. Chapter 14, "Combating Anti-Asian Hate Case Study Workshop," provides a professional development plan on how to respond to Anti-Asian hate in the moment. This will be especially helpful to whoever leads explicit racial justice professional development (if you don't have that person, please reach out!). I'm a firm believer in teaching through case study practice and analysis because it helps us become an upstander when witnessing anti-Asian hate or violence. Upstanders are not passive when anti-Asian hate or violence occurs, they act! I say this many times throughout the book that racial justice lives in the body.

This ends with the final chapter, Chapter 15 entitled "Asian Americans and Abolition." Educating toward abolition is the aspiration. I recognize how difficult and impossible this may seem, as you operate within a racist system tied to colonialism and capitalism. And yes, I said it. The United States education system was founded on a racist system that continues to privilege many over others, a system meant to acculturate immigrants and strip them of their native cultures. It continues to force whiteness as the ideal, upholding the myth of meritocracy, falsely urging communities of color to assimilate in order to survive and thrive. In my poem, I end with "while they name themselves now: 'allies'" which takes on a facetious tone because this is where people tend to stop. This is the line of comfort that people, often white educators, will not cross because sustainable and long-term commitments in the form of action overwhelms them. But this is the line that we need everyone to cross and sustain in order for our communities to thrive.

Other material I've included are a glossary and reference section.

The Cadence

For navigability, I curated each chapter to have this cadence:

- ◆ The Personal Is Political
- ◆ The Praxis: Action and Reflection
- ◆ A Movement, Not a Moment

The sections called "The Personal Is Political" pay homage to bell hooks and give context as to why each chapter matters to me and why it should matter to you. This book is a manifestation of lived experiences connecting to other lived experiences nodding their heads at each other in affirmation. My lived experience intersects that of my ancestors before me. Because of the system we live in, Asian Americans can relive ethnoracial trauma just by learning about traumatic experiences. We relive ethnoracial joy and resilience through the same means. We start with the "why" because it grounds us with intention, and with intention we can drive toward the broader vision of combating anti–Asian American sentiment while embodying a pro–Asian American lens.

From there we move into Paulo Freire's concept of "Praxis," which is the cycle of action and reflection in order to sharpen our social justice lens. The section "The Praxis: Action and Reflection" in each chapter charges educators to reflect, as well as offers tangible ideas on how to incorporate the content into your classes.

Throughout each chapter there will also be reflection questions. The idea here is to get out your notebook or journals and reflect on the content you have just read. The reflection questions aim at connecting the content to your schema or previous experiences or lack thereof regarding the content.

At the end of each chapter is a section called "A Movement, Not a Moment" to help others understand that this book is a part of a movement fighting for Asian American studies and ethnic studies at large. Often, authors are seen as the topic's expert after their books are published. While I am an expert in teaching Asian American narratives, I would be remiss if I did not honor those who came before, especially those who helped influence this book project, and those who will give thoughtful feedback and critique on improving future editions.

Part 1

Teach Us Visible by Remembering Us

What Do You Know About Asian America? Self-Assessment and Framework

◆ Practitioners will assess their own knowledge of Asian America (knowledge and skill).

◆ Practitioners will learn how to assess their students' knowledge pertaining to Asian America (skill).

The Personal Is Political

In this section, you will encounter a few concepts that I tackle in this book: the perpetual foreigner stereotype, the model minority myth, and yellow peril. What you'll notice throughout Chapter 1 and throughout the book is that I always root these concepts in story because the personal is indeed political.

The Perpetual Foreigner Stereotype

"When was the first time Asian American became a political identity for you?"

I was asked this question in an interview recently. As an Asian American education-activist, you would think the answer would roll off my tongue like a question about age, but it didn't. I wanted to connect this answer to my experience organizing Asian Americans to fight for data disaggregation in Boston in 2019, or in 2012 when I first started teaching Asian American studies in

Indianapolis. But in retrospect, knowing that everything is political, I have to go back to my childhood "lunchbox moments," a time when I was reminded of my race based on the food I ate and who didn't accept me for it.

I remember bringing leftover dilis, vinegar, and rice. Dilis is like an anchovy. It was one of my favorite foods growing up, but soon it became something I avoided because students started to look at me in disgust eating food like this during lunch. I convinced my mom to buy Lunchables soon after so I would fit in. This impacted the way I valued my own culture and, thus, my identity as a Filipino American. In fact, I wrote a poem about it in *Hyphen Magazine: Asian Americans Unabridged*. I was inspired by Clint Smith's *My Jump Shot* where he uses the anaphora or repeating phrase "My Jump Shot" to talk about the stereotypes that Black boys experience. In my case, "My Lunchbox" paints a story of assimilation:

My Lunch Box (after Clint Smith)

by Tony DelaRosa

My lunchbox is transformer
My lunchbox is *Dinuguan* one day
    the dugo be the chocolate sauce of the pig
    the ritual words most Filipino parents abused
    to conceal the truth behind a slaughter
My lunchbox is *Dilis* the next day
    the *Whoever Smelt It, Dealt It* finger-fish
    with the side of vinegar dip
My lunchbox is an homage to *sawsawan*
My lunchbox is an entire conversation with one *kamay*
My lunchbox is "my momma did that" *(pointing to its ribcage, while*
    grains of rice celestial to each finger)
My lunchbox is transformer though
My lunchbox is Greek mythology in the Midwest
My lunchbox is forming crop circles
One day, my lunchbox made Bobby's face cringe into
his Wonder Bread

and made Chris' nose fall off like the Sphinx
while Felix escaped into his Lunchable
My lunchbox is unlovable, urban legend, Unesco
World Heritage site forgotten
My lunchbox is wishing for a new mouth: new
teeth, new tongue, new breath, new lungs
My lunchbox is everyone's "yuck my yum"
My lunchbox is transforming full moon
My lunchbox is having surgery again,
     the doctors say that we only have to pay on
the front end
My lunchbox knew that was a lie, but went
Optimus Prime anyway ...
My lunchbox is Lunchable in a minute
My Lunchable is lovable now
     it wears plastic like a Ken Doll
     its ribcage, a bento box of Ritz Crackers
     and Kraft Singles
My Lunchable is *American Born Chinese*
My Lunchable is David Blaine carrying itself with
no handles
     levitating into a dream
       where Chris' nose magically reappeared
       where Bobby's face smiled
         my forbearance on fleek,
         as if the latter
           always was,
         as if everyone was
         so forgiving.

The concept of lunchbox moments is not new, but it is rarely understood outside of the Asian American community or broader immigrant community. While these lunchbox moments are not what activated me to become an activist in education, they are origin stories to me understanding the "perpetual foreigner" stereotype. This is the idea that Asian Americans will always be seen as foreigners no matter how hard we assimilate into white dominant culture. The perpetual foreigner is one of the main concepts that this book teaches educators how to identify and combat in schools.

> **REFLECTION QUESTION**
>
> Where have you seen the perpetual foreigner stereotype in your educational experience?

The Model Minority Myth

Another concept that you'll see spiraling throughout these chapters is the model minority myth. If you're a socially active Asian American, this term is not new to you. If you're a Person of Color (PoC), this term may also not be new to you. For the white teachers reading this book, my hope is that this is not new to you, and if it is, then this book will ensure that this term is no longer seen as "new" or "jargony."

The *model minority myth* phrase dates back to the 1940s around the time the Chinese Exclusion Act was repealed. It was at a time when the United States viewed Chinese Americans as a model citizen in relation to Japanese Americans, who were seen as "bad" because of the beginnings of World War II. During this time, China was an ally, and Japan was the enemy. Eventually, in the 1970s, the model minority evolved to center Japanese Americans as model citizens relative to the Black community, who were seen as the "problem minorities." This term has been used as a tool for anti-Blackness, driving a wedge between the Asian American and Black communities.

An example of this concept of wedging can manifest in how Asian American students versus Black students get seen in schools. Oftentimes, Asian American students are seen as "self-reliant," "good at STEM," or inherently "hardworking," whereas Black students are seen as "not self-reliant," "not good at STEM," or inherently "lazy." These vastly different perceptions and stereotypes can cause wedging because Asian Americans who internalize the model minority myth may inherently think they perform better than Black students, which is not true. The model minority myth erases histories of systemic racism and its impacts on the Black community versus the Asian community. It erases potential bridges for Asian Americans and the Black community to connect and build solidarity. Some of these bridges are stories of immigration, stories of overlapping oppression, stories of resistance, stories of joy, and more.

The model minority myth continues to impact the Asian American community with ongoing stereotypes such as the following statements:

"Asian Americans are good at STEM subjects."	"Asian Americans are rich."	"Asian Americans are hardworking."
"Asian Americans are docile and submissive."	"Asian Americans don't complain."	"Asian Americans are spiritually enlightened."
"Asian Americans are self-reliant."	"Asian Americans don't have mental health concerns."	"Asian Americans are living the American dream."
"Asian Americans don't experience racism."	"Asian Americans only live within affluent communities."	"Asian Americans are white-adjacent."

REFLECTION QUESTIONS

Which of these statements have you heard before?

Which one(s) of these did you believe to be true and why?

Unfortunately, because the model minority myth is a product of white supremacy, it will not be gone anytime soon. However, we can continue to combat it as it shows up and create systems and cultures that paint a more holistic narrative of who we are as a diverse community.

Yellow Peril and the "Asian Menace"

Yellow peril is the concept of seeing Asian Americans and Asians as a menace to society. This first started in the late 1800s, when white working-class laborers who were fearful of losing their jobs during economic crisis scapegoated Chinese people calling them "filthy yellow hordes." This bled into the 1882 Chinese Exclusion Act, which prohibited immigration from China and forbade current Chinese Americans from becoming citizens.

Later this concept of "Asian menace" was applied to the Japanese during the 1904–05 Russo-Japanese War. Again, we would see the Yellow Peril concept after the Japanese attack on Pearl Harbor. The Japanese were portrayed as subhuman apes, treacherous, and physically and mentally lesser than Americans. At this time, the model minority myth was applied to Chinese and Chinese Americans because they were seen as allies to the United States, and in Frank Chin's words they experienced "racist love"—the concept of being loved for being an ally to another enemy but still experiencing unique racism for not being American (Chin, 1972).

Beyond yellow peril, Asian Americans have been seen as a "menace" to society in other forms. Beginning on January 19, 1930, mobs of up to 500 white people including police attacked Filipino farmworkers and their property after Filipino men were seen dancing with white women. For another example, look no further than September 11, 2001, when the twin towers were struck by terrorist attacks. Directly after September 11, 2001, the Sikh Coalition received thousands of reports from the Sikh community about hate crimes, workplace discrimination, school bullying, and racial and religious profiling.

REFLECTION QUESTION

Where do we see instances of yellow peril or "Asians as menace" today?

Combating the perpetual foreigner stereotype, the model minority myth, and yellow peril/Asian as menace begins with interrogating our knowledge, mindsets, and ways of being toward Asian Americans. Once we are able to identify where we see these three concepts manifest on the micro and macro levels, we start to develop our pro–Asian American lens. In the next section, you'll be introduced to a self-assessment that will help you know where you can start on your journey.

The Self-Assessment

In 2020, I led a national online panel called "Isang Bagsak as Verb." This is a series I co-founded that started with a panel on Black and

Filipino American solidarity in schools. This panel was spurred by the death of George Floyd and the rise of anti–Asian American hate and violence across the country because Asians and Asian Americans were being scapegoated as the cause of the COVID-19 pandemic. One of our panelists was Dr. Liza Talusan (she/her), author of the *Identity Conscious Educator*, and someone I look up to. One thing Dr. Talusan said stuck out to me:

> *"When I did my doctoral dissertation surveying educators across the country about what they knew in regard to Asian American history, the same four concepts came up: 1) that Pearl Harbor happened, 2) that Chinese people built the railroads, 3) that there were Japanese internment camps, and 4) that there was a war in Vietnam."*

This signals a crisis in our education system and is one of the many reasons why we continue to see harmful stereotypes and violence toward Asian Americans today. If educators can remember only four main events that intersect war and indentured servitude, how can educators teach our history and narratives with nuance and care?

I added the assessment in the following section "The Praxis: Action and Reflection" to help educators have a starting place to reflect, since that is the first part of praxis. In bold you'll see the purpose of each question. These questions are a mixture of identifying how much you know about Asian American narratives, Asian American impact, how often you learned about Asian Americans, how often you taught about Asian Americans, and interrogating the why behind all of this. Getting to the root of these questions helps you understand your socialization. When you pull at the root of how you have been socialized to view Asian Americans, this opens a path to an abolitionist lens.

The beauty of this assessment is that it can also be used with your students or other educators should you lead people in anti-bias and anti-racist educational work. In the next section, you'll encounter the adult practitioner and student versions of the assessment.

The Praxis: Action and Reflection

Practitioner Version

Take this version yourself to understand where you stand with regard to Asian American history:

Understand yourself in relation to Asian American social movements.

Q: Without looking this up, name five Asian American social movements in US history.

Help you understand how much you know about Asian American impact (past and present).

Q: Without looking this up, name five Asian American leaders and their impact on society.

Q: How many of these five Asian American leaders are Southeast Asian, South Asian, have a disability, or identify as LGBTQIA+

Understand where you are as a teacher in being inclusive of Asian Americans in your lesson plans.

Q: When was the last time you taught anything Asian American in your classroom?

Q: Was it only during May's Asian Pacific Islander American Heritage Month? Was it during Filipino American History Month? Why or why not?

Understand the reasons.

Q: So far, reflect on why or why you have not incorporated Asian American history and narratives into your teaching?

Q: What questions do you have about Asian America?

Student Version

Give this quick assessment to your students to understand where they are when it comes to Asian American history. This assessment is not aimed at invoking shame within students for not knowing the "correct" answer. Sometimes shame tied to the concept of perfectionism can manifest when students take tests, so framing this as a generative process of learning what we know and don't know is important. Have them answer to the best of their abilities.

1. Can you name five or more Asian American leaders in the US?
2. I know the difference between East Asian, West Asian, Southeast Asian, and South Asian.
3. When was the last time you learned about Asian American history?
4. Are Asians and Asian Americans the same? Yes/No
5. What questions do you have about Asian America?

After this assessment, you can have group discussions with students on what was challenging about this assessment and why. Asking "why" helps students think about where they get their knowledge of Asian Americans. This follow-up can lead into the generative discussion of why current sources of Asian American education (i.e., movies and pop culture), are limiting and why we need Asian American history education.

A Movement, Not a Moment

Here are a few resources I often go to help strengthen my lens into Asian America as it pertains to education. I chose each resource here where I learned a broad range of Asian American issues since this is the first chapter. In subsequent chapters, you'll start to see that the resources I add are more nuanced because the topics start to zoom in on specific ideas pertaining to Asian America.

TITLE/LINKS	AUTHOR(S)	WHAT'S IN THIS RESOURCE?
Teaching about Asian Pacific Americans: Effective Activities, Strategies, and Assignments for Classrooms and Communities	Edith Wen-Chu Chen and Glenn Omatsu	This resource offers ready to go activities, strategies, and assignments.
The Making of Asian America	Erika Lee	This resource offers a deep history of how Asian America came to be.

(Continues)

(Continued)

TITLE/LINKS	AUTHOR(S)	WHAT'S IN THIS RESOURCE?
Minor Feelings	Cathy Park Hong	This resource is an autobiography of essays reflecting on Asian American identity.
Strangers from a Different Shore	Ronald Takaki	This resource offers narrative history, personal recollection, and oral testimonies on Asian American history.
Contemporary Asian American Activism: Building Movements for Liberation	Diane C. Fujino and Robyn Magalit Rodriguez	This resource offers essays on today's Asian American activist movements.

Chapter 2

Windows, Mirrors, and Sliding Glass Doors Framework

LEARNING OBJECTIVES

◆ Practitioners will understand the concepts of windows, mirrors, and sliding glass doors and apply them to their practice (knowledge).

◆ Practitioners will reflect on their identity, intersectionality, and broader positionality as it pertains to Asian American narratives (skill).

The Personal Is Political

Will they style us windows and pick up a mirror?

I wrote this line in the opening poem to charge educators to think about their positionality in relation to racial equity. Author Luis Sánchez describes positionality as:

"The notion that personal values, views, and location in time and space influence how one understands the world. In this context, gender, race, class, and other aspects of identities are indicators of social and spatial positions and are not fixed, given qualities. Positions act on the knowledge a person has about things, both material and abstract. Consequently, knowledge is the product of a specific position that reflects particular places and spaces."

The window, mirrors, and sliding glass doors framework, pioneered by Emily Styles and Rudine Sims Bishop, helps us think about our positionality concerning another identity marker or set of identity markers and for this book, I'd ask you to think about your ethnic or racial identity concerning Asian Americans. I first stumbled upon this theory when I taught students spoken word poetry. In 2013, I was teaching at Indianapolis Public School 103, which was an elementary school. When no one at my school had a clue about Asian Pacific Islander American Heritage Month or the acronym APIA, I wanted to change that. I focused on my students and shared the narratives of Asian American poets such as: Beau Sia, Franny Choi, Nick Carbó, and Leah Lakshmi Piepzna-Samarasinha.

Since my students were mostly African Americans, I wanted to prepare the lesson around the value of learning from different cultures and perspectives, which is a deep part of culturally relevant and sustaining teaching (CRST) coined and founded by Dr. Gloria Ladson-Billings, aka "The Notorious Dr. GLB." To Dr. GLB's concept of strengthening my students' sociopolitical consciousness, I kept thinking to myself, "How are they going to be holistic and intentional global citizens if they are not exposed to the world beyond their zip codes?" I wanted to ensure that they had the best tools presented to them to access nuanced narratives of the Asian American diaspora.

I had another opportunity to concretize this framework as a teaching fellow for Dr. Josephine Kim's Race, Ethnicity, and Culture: Contemporary Issues in Asian America course at the Harvard Graduate School of Education. Instead of PK–12 students, I worked to educate, guide, and assess graduate students from all ethnoracial backgrounds in navigating this course through the Windows and Mirrors framework. Starting the course with the Windows and Mirrors framework helped center the voices of Asian American students while participating.

Finally, this brings us to the "door." People have referred to this concept as "the sliding glass door," which forces participants to imagine themselves in the world of others. I don't want readers to confuse this with cultural tourism, but rather a way of being in community with Asian Americans. I want to shift the lens and push the rigor here and move from input to outputs or actions that make your pro–Asian Americanness unconditional. In a society that obsesses over book clubs and social media, learning and sharing social media posts is still surface level in comparison to sustainable action.

My charge for you is to challenge your students to get active in their own communities as it pertains to Asian Americans. Think of the door with regard to Bloom's Taxonomy, where you are pushing kids to not only "remember" facts and information about Asian Americans, but also to push themselves to critically "understand," "analyze," and "evaluate" our issues. This will enable them to "apply" and "create" ways in their own communities on how to embody a pro–Asian American lens, whether it means researching Asian American narratives or inviting Asian American community members to share their gifts or stories with the school.

As you approach this book, thinking about your positionality is critical for success. Like many anti-bias and anti-racist books, it really starts with the self. Chinese American activist Grace Lee Boggs once said, "We must transform ourselves to transform the world." I want you to take that lens as you approach this chapter and the book. Think about this quote as, "We must transform ourselves to transform the world we offer in our classrooms."

To dive deeper into the Windows, Mirrors, and Sliding Glass Doors framework, here's one way you can approach your classroom:

◆ Question if you're approaching this book from the lens of an Asian American?

  If so, from which ethnicity are you approaching it? Do you have any other salient identities that drive the way you read books? If you are of the Asian American diaspora but are not socialized to embrace that identity, why is that? How can this book help you embrace and reclaim your version of an Asian American identity?

◆ If you're non–Asian American POC, then you are looking through this through both a window and mirror depending on how you relate to the content presented.

◆ If you're white, then you are looking at this book and Asian American narratives through the window.

I want to stress the incompleteness of what I just shared. It is difficult and, in fact, unnatural to isolate identities, especially if you are constantly thinking of multiple identities at the same time. What I shared is just an example of how you can leverage the

Windows, Mirrors, and Sliding Glass Door theory from a self-perspective. We can all "open doors" to help Asian Americans even when you are nowhere near. And that's the point, we need educators who are teaching in areas that don't have a high concentration of Asian Americans, or none at all, to pay attention and embrace a pro–Asian American lens. This is that unconditional love for intersectional social justice I mentioned in the beginning of the book. After the learning and reflection, what's next for you and your classroom?

The Praxis: Action and Reflection

Before we begin looking at a step-by-step process leveraging the Windows, Mirrors, and Sliding Glass Doors framework in class, I want to share a caveat around the framing; you want to ensure that your framing doesn't involve the famous saying: reading lets you escape to different places. Educator and instructional coach Terry Kawi argues that this saying emphasizes that some places are bad or good, which can implicitly lead to xenophobia. When framing this technique, lean into curiosity. You can say that this is a method that helps us understand ourselves as global citizens and allows us to understand our histories in relation to other people's histories.

We are not trying to promote cultural tourism or voyeurism, the idea that you visit and tour a foreign country; we are trying to help our students understand global solidarity with Asians and Asian Americans.

Example of Windows, Mirrors, and Sliding Glass Doors Framework

After your framing, let's look at an example of how I would teach this concept in a step-by-step process similar to a poetry lesson. Here are a few steps I would take:

1. Introduce the Windows, Mirrors, and Sliding Door concept.

2. Activate prior knowledge by having students conduct research around the author and the title of a poem. In this case, I suggest using a poem called *My Filipino*, which I got published in a zine sponsored by Asian Americans Advancing Justice Atlanta.

3. Have students compare and contrast their identities with the authors' identities. Through a Venn diagram, I had them find similarities and differences.

STUDENT IDENTITY	SIMILARITIES	AUTHOR IDENTITY

4. Have students read the texts two or more times: 1) once for a broad understanding and to reflect on their immediate reactions, and 2) another round for a close reading to get to the technicalities of the poem (i.e., literary devices and structure).

Personally, I like to charge students to read a third time to get another overall understanding of the poem based on what they have uncovered. There is always room for new interpretations to arise.

5. After the readings, assess students by asking the following:

a. What was a mirror for you?

b. What was a window for you?

c. What doors can we open from this reading?

Step 5 can happen after each round of reading. I think this is a powerful way to assess how students are interpreting the poem. After the second or third reading, I recommend doing part c because they now should have a stronger understanding of what's at stake in the poem. Once they understand what's at stake, they are able to offer a clearer and more tangible "door."

I have added one of my poems as a mentor text that you can use with your students to try the Windows, Mirror and Sliding Glass Door activity; see https://docs.google.com/document/d/1hkgw9Bo-mTUZFt-3oNY4nJVAX_-l9iI8/edit.

My Filipino

by Tony DelaRosa after Melissa Lozada-Oliva

If you ask me if I am fluent in Filipino I will tell you
My Filipino is not my anchor, although leagues beneath me
holding its breath. My Filipino breathes in half beats,
a lung(uage) of too many tongues and too many stories to
untell. My Filipino is Cavite and Pampanga.
My Filipino is my mother and my father.
Both tongues, captains and captives
at the same shipwreck.

My Filipino is a long lost gift; the forgotten rudder
that pushes someone else's footprints starboard. In the
13th century, it was wrapped up and given a name by
the Chinese called Ma-i (country of the blacks).
In the 16th century it was wrapped up and given a
truncated name after King Philip the II. My motherland
birthed by a sun. Can't spell yourself out of hispanic
without the pronoun "his" and panicking, without
"his" and then intergenerational trauma...

Can't seem to be given a name other than el negrito
o el chinito.
To Hispanics it's a term of endearment; the diminutive,
another gift,

Fast forward, my Filipino panics in the corner of
Mr. Seibert's classroom.
My Filipino is given a new name, "Fil-Am."
Yet it knows that saying the pledge of allegiance is like double
Dutch with two left feet,
with no jump
     and all rope
          and always
               sinking.
Might as well mean Filipino - Aftermath.
After so many iterations, a name loses its north star

And a people lose directions to freedom, and people
lose a galaxy.
If you ask me if I am fluent in Filipino
All I remember is nakalimutan...
    What's left of a ghost of a ghost of a ghost of a ghost
    of a ghost?
        What happens to the host?
            Does language commandeer itself into
            doubling erasure?
            Can phantom limbs speak themselves
            back into
            Can phantom limbs speak themselves back
            Can phantom limbs speak themselves
            Can phantom limbs speak
            Can phantom limbs
            Can phantom
            or just phantom.

Sample Answers

Here are some sample answers for upper elementary and middle school:

a. What was a mirror for you?

This was a mirror because I can see how the poet is caught between multiple identities like a tug-o-war.

b. What was a window for you?

This was a window for me because this is the first time hearing about how a Filipino American feels about the origins of their name.

c. What doors can we open from this reading?

A door that I'm opening is the idea that Filipinos and other Asian Americans may be feeling a sense of "double erasure" and because of that, I can help cheer them on if they feel like they are trying to connect with their identity.

Here are some sample answers for high school:

a. What was a mirror for you?

I think a mirror for me is when the poet says, "pushing someone else footprints starboard." It makes me think about my own sense of agency over my name. It also makes me think about passivity, and how the poet is trying to say that his Filipino identity can feel like being lodged in passivity. This is similar to (insert identity) because we have been seen as a passive group due to colonization.

b. What was a window for you?

A window for me is the idea of seeing a Filipino question the origins of their name. The poet goes into how they were given names by the Chinese and the Spanish, and it begs the question about self-naming and sovereignty.

c. What doors can we open from this reading?

A door for me is to learn more about the Filipino diaspora because I didn't know about the different colonial relationships that the Philippines had with China and Spain. It makes me want to go deeper into what other colonial relationships and impacts colonization has on the Philippines, Filipinos, and Filipino Americans.

A Movement, Not a Moment

The beautiful thing about the Windows, Mirrors, and Sliding Glass Doors theory and framework is that it is helpful when teaching the narratives of other marginalized groups. To find out how others use this framework, continue your learning by visiting some of the links:

TITLE/LINKS	AUTHOR(S)	WHAT'S IN THIS RESOURCE?
Curriculum as Window and Mirror by The National Seed Project nationalseedproject.org/ Key-SEED-Texts/ curriculum-as-window- and-mirror	The National Seed Project	This resource goes deeper into understanding how curriculum can be seen as both window and mirror.
The Importance of Windows and Mirrors in Stories www.pbs.org/education/blog/ the-importance-of-windows- and-mirrors-in-stories	PBS	This resource offers helpful questions for students when switching from windows and mirrors.

TITLE/LINKS	AUTHOR(S)	WHAT'S IN THIS RESOURCE?
What are Windows, Mirrors, and Sliding Glass Doors? www.weareteachers.com/ mirrors-and-windows/	We Are Teachers	This resource offers more information on the sliding glass door, as well as pushes teachers to expand this framework to every school subject.
Window or Mirror? by Learning for Justice www.learningforjustice.org/ classroom-resources/ teaching-strategies/close-and-critical-reading/ window-or-mirror	Learning for Justice	This resource offers a lesson plan to teach the concept of windows and mirrors.

Chapter 3

Timeline of Anti–Asian American Racism and Violence

LEARNING OBJECTIVES:

◆ Practitioners will learn about the history of anti–Asian American racism and violence (knowledge).

◆ Practitioners will learn how to build knowledge and inspire reflection on anti–Asian American racism and violence as it pertains to today's Stop Asian Hate movement (skill).

Content Warning: In this chapter, I chronologically outline policies, practices, and moments that symbolize anti–Asian American racism and violence. Researching and writing about this brought up a lot of strong emotions and reminded me of traumatic experiences. If reading about moments of trauma pertaining to Asian Americans and broadly marginalized people impacts you in a similar way, please do what you need to do to prepare yourself for this chapter.

The Personal Is Political

During the rise of anti-Asian hate and violence in 2020 because Asians and Asian Americans were scapegoated for causing the pandemic, I have been gaslighted to believe that these hate crimes that have risen to the thousands, (according to the organization Stop AAPI Hate) only began in 2020. As someone who has faced anti–Asian American sentiment through verbal and physical attacks and knows of other Asian Americans who have, it has been helpful to know the sources of some of these racist issues. As a boy in middle and high school, I was bullied and jumped by other kids of all races because of their ignorance. I was often greeted with "ching chong ching chong" or "stupid Puerto Rican ch*nk." People fear what they cannot name, and that fear can turn into violence. The gaslighting was often reinforced by those same peers celebrating my resilience during all of it. They would say, "Tony, you're so tough for an Asian kid" or "this Brown Asian kid is from the street, he can take licks." Unfortunately, growing up I saw this type of "celebrating resilience instead of tackling root causes that require resilience" all throughout our society. I want to amplify Dr. E.J. David Ramos's sentiments:

> *"The problem is not our resilience but a world that constantly requires our resilience, and a world that has come to learn that our resilience is permission for our continued oppression."*

As you read the following timeline, know that in Chapter 4, I will also highlight the moments that have benefitted Asian Americans through history's policy and events to focus on the progress that we have achieved.

This chapter outlines a linear timeline that points to specific laws, policies, and events that contribute to the hate and violence we see today.

Timeline

- ◆ **1790 Federal Naturalization Law:** An 18th century law that served as the foundation for racial discrimination in naturalization rulings. It limited naturalization of foreign-born people to "white" people only.

- ◆ **1854 People vs. Hall:** A supreme court case showed that Chinese people were not allowed to testify in court (like Black and Native Americans).

- ◆ **1875 Page Act:** The Act that barred Chinese women from entering the United States for being accused of spreading diseases and promiscuity.

- ◆ **1882 Chinese Exclusion Act:** The largest act to ban Chinese from immigrating to the United States ending in 1943 with the Magnuson Act.

◆ **1905 Japanese & Korean Exclusion League:** An organization in California that evolved into the Asiatic Exclusion League to prevent interracial relationships with people of Asian descent.

◆ **1906 Programme for Patriotic Exercises in the Public Schools in Hawaii:** An intentional policy to obliterate the national consciousness of the Hawaiian kingdom in schools.

◆ **1923 US vs. Bhagat Singh Thind:** A case involving a Punjabi immigrant who married a white woman, became a US citizen, and served for a time in World War I. He applied for naturalization, but the United States ruled he was not defined as "white," therefore denying him naturalization.

◆ **1920–1930s Watsonville Anti-Filipino Riots:** An event led by 500 white men and supported by the police attacking Filipino farm workers seen dancing with white women.

◆ **1942–1945 Executive Order 9066:** An order issued by President Franklin D. Roosevelt forced Japanese Americans into internment camps, accusing them of potential espionage.

◆ **1965 Hart-Cellar Act:** An act signed by President Lyndon B. Johnson, which targeted Asian, Latino/a/x, and African migrants; shifting immigration from an exclusionary quota system to a merit-based points system.

◆ **1974 Lau vs. Nichols:** A landmark 1974 Supreme Court decision aimed to make school transition easier for young people who speak English as their second language.

◆ **1998–2016 Southeast Asian deportations based on criminal convictions:** 14,000 Southeast Asian refugees from Vietnam, Laos, and Cambodia are living in limbo as they await deportation orders.

◆ **2001 Brown Asian American Scapegoating:** After the attacks on September 11, 2001, there was an increase of racial discrimination and violence toward Sikh, Muslim, and South Asian/Desi Americans.

◆ **2006 Fong Lee Incident:** Fong Lee (19) was a Hmong teen who was shot eight times and killed at the hands of Minneapolis police for allegedly having a gun. His family believes the gun was planted. The police officer was acquitted by an all-white jury and awarded a medal.

- ◆ **2012 Murder of Sikh Americans:** In Oak Creek, Wisconsin, a white terrorist murdered six Sikh Americans at a Sikh temple, mistaking them for Muslims. In this case, the Sikh Americans identified as Punjabi.

- ◆ **2019 Nepalese Fight for TPS:** In 2019, the Trump administration conducted an unlawful termination of temporary protected status for Nepalese and Honduran people.

- ◆ **2021 Atlanta Shootings:** Four Korean and two Chinese American women were killed in a hate crime, while police say the white identifying murderer was having a "bad day."

- ◆ **2021 Indianapolis Shootings:** Four Sikh people were killed at a FedEx facility. People are still debating if this was a hate crime, even when 90% of the people who worked there identified as Sikh.

Whew. Take a deep breath because this is traumatic. Take a deep breath for the Asian Americans who were targeted in these laws, policies, and events. With the fight for Asian American studies and history on the rise in this country, it is equally important to have an ongoing reference list to always put our lives into historical context. Yes, we have faced and continue to face racism. A residual of racism is anti–Asian American hate and violence.

Praxis: Action and Reflection

In this work, understanding that Asian Americans are historically impacted by racist policies is important in holding our narratives with care and equity. To most of you, this content is probably new since it is not taught in PreK–12 classrooms. Pull out your journal and answer the following questions to the best of your abilities.

Activity 1: Self

1. Out of these incidents and policies, which is sticking with you most and why?

2. Which of these incidents and policies have had the most impact on the Asian American community? Why?

3. What incidents or policies would you add that are not included here?

4. What do you believe would be different for you if you had known about these incidents and policies?

Activity 2: Students

Similar to you, unless this knowledge was passed on by family or your student has a strong sense of identity and history, this information will be new. Since most of your students are probably building their container of knowledge around these events, here are a few activities you can propose:

- ◆ **Jigsaw:** Print out articles associated with these policies and issues. Have students read them in assigned pairings or groups, and after 30 minutes, have them take turns presenting the content, sharing summaries of the events, and how they connected to them.

- ◆ **Research:** Assign these issues and policies to students, and have them practice researching these topics and creating a presentation on what they learned by using Prezi, PowerPoint, Informal Poster, or Flip Grid.

- ◆ **Interview:** Print out this list of topics and have students interview a family member with regard to how they view the policy or incident.

- ◆ **Recreate:** Have students recreate the timeline, and have them find specific people associated with a particular incident or policy.

Activity 3: School

Some of you are ready to assume the work of informing others at your school on how to view through a pro–Asian American lens. One way you can do this at your school is to lead a discussion with school faculty and staff. Print out the timeline, post it in a large room, and have participants conduct their own chalk walk in reflecting on these incidents. Following the chalk walk, have everyone read reflections, and then hold a partner and whole group discussion on how this timeline was received.

After the faculty and staff-facing discussion, challenge school faculty to build in class time or advisory to have a similar discussion with their students. The work always starts with us. When we're more prepared to have discussions around embodying a pro–Asian American lens and combating anti-Asian racism and violence, then this will build the container for a pro–Asian American school.

A Movement, Not a Moment

There are so many available and valuable online timelines that are underused. The previous timeline focuses on systems, policies, and incidents. The following is a list of more timelines that I often use in my human development with schools and private companies to teach about the systemic impacts of incidents and policies that negatively impact Asian Americans.

TITLE/LINKS	AUTHOR(S)	WHAT'S IN THIS RESOURCE?
A Different Asian American Timeline aatimeline.com	ChangeLab	This online resource focuses on logics that shape racial stratification and group-differentiated access to power in the modern world.
11 Moments in Asian American History You Should Know time.com/5956943/ aapi-history-milestones	*Time Magazine*	This resource focuses on 11 events, policies, and milestones in Asian American History recounted by Asian American scholars and activists.
Asian American Timeline by Dr. Bonnie Khaw-Posthuma www.chaffey.edu/spops/docs/ asian-american-timeline.pdf	Dr. Bonnie Khaw-Posthuma	This resource is a four-page printout of events, policies, and milestones in Asian American History.
Asian American History by University of Pennsylvania School of Arts and Sciences www.sas.upenn.edu/~rle/ History.html	Asian American Studies Program	This resource links to UPenn's Asian American studies program including a timeline and resources for teachers.

Chapter 4

Timeline of Pro–Asian American Milestones and Permissions

LEARNING OBJECTIVES:

- ◆ Participants will learn about the history of Asian American resistance and milestones that followed (knowledge).

- ◆ Participants will learn the difference between "extractive" and "just" storytelling (knowledge and mindset).

- ◆ Participants will learn how to teach Asian American timelines in both Chapters 3 and 4 (skill).

The Personal Is Political

Will they play our battle drums?
Will they plant our Chrysanthemums?

In Chapter 3, you read about laws, policies, and moments in history that reflect the institutional and systemic ways anti-Asian racism, violence, and sentiment manifests in the United States. In this chapter, I charge you to think about how you plan to play our battle drums and plant our Chrysanthemums for students and staff in your school by understanding some laws, policies, and moments in history that reflect the milestones won by Asian Americans.

This metaphor of a battle drum and a Chrysanthemum can symbolize Asian American battles won and ways of securing our well-being. I want to underscore that these milestones wouldn't be considered notable milestones if the status quo was not racist and exclusionary toward Asians and Asian Americans. For this same reason, I also add the term "permissions," invoking this concept of the oppressor or gatekeeper giving up their power in order for the Asian American community to feel included. Thus, the pro–Asian American aspect of providing this timeline focuses on resistance, accomplishment, and access to power in spite of oppression between the 1700s and the 1980s. Later in the book, I will continue referencing moments in the 1990s and on to help expand on moments of pro–Asian American sentiment.

As an educator who curates critical educational material regarding Asian American studies, it's difficult to shift from a deficit to a positive lens regarding Asian America, because the oppression can feel like all encompassing with what the media chooses to amplify and the nature of being a critical scholar. Let me expand on both points.

From a media standpoint, the trap of getting invested in witnessing and sharing Asian American trauma is both perverse and a product of capitalism. The term "trauma porn" comes to mind. Black Public Media dispatch writer Leslie Fields-Cruz describes trauma porn as the following:

"A recurring element of Extractive Storytelling. The media's excuse for distributing such graphic images is that it "raises public awareness." But for those at the center of these stories, the footage is nothing short of the digital embalming of their most agonizing and humiliating moments." (2021)

This is where Chapter 2 on mirrors, windows, and sliding glass doors is helpful in understanding if you are participating in extractive storytelling or in what Sonya Childress explains as "Just Storytelling," a filmmaking ethos that is locally grounded, healing-focused, antiracist, and in conversation with justice movements. Some questions Childress poses to lean into Just Storytelling are the following:

◆ What is your personal connection or unique vantage point to the story?

◆ How might you mitigate your biases or knowledge limitations that may impact the storytelling?

◆ Who can you partner with to inform your understanding of the issue or community?

- How will you ensure your teaching of the story is equitable, ethical, and antiracist?
- How will your teaching honor and have the true consent of the people at the center of the story?

A theme of "Just Storytelling" emphasizes the teacher's positionality to the Asian American narrative they are trying to tell. It underscores the ethics of storytelling and charges the teacher to reconsider what consent means.

Outside of choosing alternatives to trauma porn and extractive storytelling, being a critical scholar can often feel like we overemphasize oppression while doing anti-oppressive work. One of my students in my 2015 poetry club reminded me of this exact problem. I wrote an entire poetry curriculum focusing on teaching students about the trauma of other marginalized communities, not realizing what effect it would have on them long term. My poets then produced poems primarily that put their trauma on display. They performed them on stages like Harvard, Yale, and TEDex. Some may argue that writing about trauma is a form of turning pain into purpose, and others may argue that this is just another form of trauma porn. Regardless, during that year, my poets were exposed to poems that facilitated different aspects of their story of self and community such as success, cross-coalition, joy, and expansiveness. Embracing a pro–Asian American lens in schools is to ensure that we know a more holistic story of Asian Americans and tell these stories justly.

The following is a timeline of historical milestones that center Asian Americans:

- **1781 Los Angeles Founder:** Antonio Miranda of the Philippines is one of the 46 founders of the present day Los Angeles.
- **1847 First Chinese Graduate:** Three Chinese students arrive in New York City for schooling. One of them, Yung Wing, graduated from Yale in 1854, becoming the first Chinese to graduate in the US.
- **1903 Japanese Mexican Labor Association Forms:** JMLA is one of the first labor coalitions with different races.

This coalition organized the sugar beet workers strike in Oxnard, CA.

◆ **1909 Japanese Workers Strike in Oahu:** The strike of 7,000 workers that lasted for four months led to the Hawaiian Sugar Planters' Association raising wages and abolishing the setting of wages by nationality.

◆ **1911 Sikh Organizing:** Sandar Baskha Singh and Jawala Singh form and organize a society of Sikhs, eventually fundraising to build a Gurdwara in 1912.

◆ **1919 Korean Women's Patriotic League forms.**

◆ **1923 Filipino boxer:** Francisco Guilledo became world flyweight champion.

◆ **1933 Alaskan Filipino-led union:** A union formed between the Cannery Workers' and Farm Labors' Union Local 18257. Founders Virgil S. Duyungan and Aurelio Simon were murdered but their legacy lives on.

◆ **1940 Bruce Lee is born.**

◆ **1943 Hazel Lee:** The first Asian American female pilot joins the WASP (Women Airforce Service Pilots) as a Chinese American.

◆ **1943 End of the Chinese Exclusion Act of 1882:** Chinese were granted naturalization.

◆ **1946 Carlos Busolan:** writes *America Is in the Heart*, which is often acknowledged as the start of the Asian American Literary Movement.

◆ **1952 Eugene Huu-Chau Trinh:** Vietnamese American astronaut is born.

◆ **1952 McCarran-Walter Immigration Nationality Act:** The act, also known as the McCarran-Walter Act, abolishes the Asiatic Barred Zone but limits immigration through quotas and creates a preference system that determines eligibility by skill sets and family ties to the US.

◆ **1969 Ethnic Studies Department:** In March 1969, President Hitch authorized the establishment of the first Ethnic Studies

Department in the country established at Berkeley due to student organizing and protests.

◆ **1977 Southeast Asian:** refugees allowed to become permanent residents.

◆ **1983 Subrahmanyan Chandrasekhar:** wins the Nobel Prize in Physics.

◆ **1984 Growing Cambodian population**: results in the erection of a Buddhist temple in Lowell, MA.

Similar to the timeline of anti–Asian American sentiment, this pro–Asian American milestone timeline is not exhaustive. My reflection questions that follow charge you to think about what patterns and questions come up after reading through this list.

Praxis: Action and Reflection

Because our country has such an overemphasis on trauma and oppression, the content in the previous timeline most likely will be new to you, especially if you do not have any proximity to Asian American experiences and narratives. Providing this alternative timeline to the anti-Asian sentiment timeline can set the stage for how students and staff in schools reflect on both the ongoing oppression coupled with Asian American resistance. Understanding that resistance is integral to characterizing Asian Americans is important in combating the model minority myth stereotype. Because the structures of Chapters 3 and 4 are interwoven, I offer similar reflection activities here to move us from reflection to action.

Activity 1: Self

1. Out of these milestones and permissions, which is sticking with you most and why?

2. Which of these milestones and permissions have had the most impact on the Asian American community? Why? Do you notice any patterns?

3. What milestones and permissions not included here would you add?

4. What do you think would have been different for you if you would have known about these milestones or permissions?

Activity 2: For Students and Staff

Now that you have both timelines, this could be a great opportunity to understand patterns of policy, impact, and the response from Asian Americans and the United States government.

The following are a few activities you can try with your students and staff:

◆ **Self-Reflection through Chalk Walk:** This activity is meant to build a broad understanding of Asian American movements and milestones.

    a. Print out this timeline and post it in your classroom or in an open space.

    b. Ask participants to chalk walk by annotating for questions to at least three to five moments on the timeline.

    c. After 20 minutes, hold a group discussion on these questions.

◆ **Storyboard:** This activity is meant to build a deep understanding and to go deeper into picking one specific moment in history. Much of what I presented in the timelines in Chapters 3 and 4 highlight a moment in time, but in reality these moments in time embody so much context.

    a. Print out this timeline and delegate a moment in time to a participant or group of participants.

    b. The individual or group can start researching the context in which this moment or milestone exists. Questions you can pose to participants are: What else was happening to other communities at this time? Who was directly involved in this moment or milestone? If we were to create these in a movie, how could we chunk the events that make up this milestone or moment?

    c. Provide students with paper and allow them to break the milestone or moment into smaller parts (I suggest four to eight slides).

    d. Present their storyboards to the class.

◆ **Comparative Analysis:** This activity is meant to make use of the anti–Asian American timeline in Chapter 3. Separating the timelines into separate foci allows us to understand different temporal stories. Bringing these two timelines together lets participants shift from "understanding" to "analysis," which is more rigorous and opens an arena for more nuanced discussion around the patterns of policy, impact, and movements.

    a. Print out both timelines and post them in an open space for participants to read.

    b. Charge them to find patterns in policy and impact. This comparative analysis forces students to understand the magnaminty of a policy or milestone on the Asian American community.

◆ **Imagining a New Future:** In the past, after teaching students about policies like the Chinese Exclusion Act, I would charge them to imagine a new future by reflecting on what could be true if, say, a policy like the Chinese Exclusion Act of 1882 or Asiatic Barred Zone was never in place. What if naturalization was never restricted? What if Asian Americans did not have quotas? What if Asian Americans were free to immigrate and settle in the United States without a price? This activity forces participants to practice their radical imagination, the concept of focusing on what could be and should be true for Asian Americans.

A Movement, Not a Moment

There are so many available and valuable online timelines that are underused. In developing the timelines in Chapters 3 and 4, I sourced material from the following three resources. These are timelines that I often use in my human development with schools and private companies to teach about the systemic impacts of incidents and policies that impact Asian Americans:

Title/Link	Author(s)	What's in This Resource?
Leadership Education for Asian Pacifics (LEAP) www.leap.org	LEAP	This resource connects practitioners to the organization that created a robust Asian American timeline. Much of what I used in both timelines in Chapters 3 and 4 reference their timeline. Reach out to this organization to request the timeline.
24 Important Milestones in Asian American History mom.com/impact/ important-milestones-in-asian-american-history	Laura Lambert	This resource briefly describes in chronological order 24 milestones in Asian American History from the Asian American leaders ascending to leadership to highlighting laws that impact our community.
A Time for Justice–A Civil Rights Timeline www.learningforjustice .org/classroom-resources/ lessons/a-time-for-justice-a-civil-rights-timeline	Learning for Justice	This resource offers a lesson plan that helps teachers teach a timeline of Civil Rights milestones centering on the Black experience. Participants can fill in the gaps to see where Asian Americans fit into this picture.

Part 2

Teach Us Visible by Centering Us

Chapter 5

Intersectionality, Plurality, and Asian Americans

LEARNING OBJECTIVES:

◆ Participants will define intersectionality and why it matters (knowledge and mindset).

◆ Participants will learn of ways to teach intersectionality centering on Asian Americans (skill).

The Personal Is Political

And what will teachers do with us?
"Fastest growing racial group"
48 countries deep
2300+ languages
(not including dialects for days)

These lines in my poem explain the vastness of the Asian diaspora. When I think *48 countries deep*, I think about the racism and irony of viewing Asian Americans as a monolith. We are a prism of identities that are ever-changing. As someone who studied Asian and Asian American studies, I am still learning about new narratives within our massive community. This is why my charge for teachers is to teach us outside of the Black and white binary.

The Black and white binary (or paradigm) is the theory that race is a concept that exists within the realm of Black and white identities. My task for you is to start including Asian Americans in your conversations about race, especially if you don't teach Asian American students. There is a misconception that "if I don't teach Asian American students, then there's no need for me to teach about Asian American narratives." I've heard this in conversation between colleagues, as well as in spaces with senior leaders in education who would say, "Asian Americans are merely guests in our spaces" (spaces focused on people of color).

This is harmful to us because it homogenizes us. It paints the trope that Asian Americans don't experience racism. Teaching with a Black and white binary lens is harmful because it can lead to lateral oppression (oppression across racial demographics) or "oppression olympics" where oppressed groups compare their oppressions within a hierarchy of who's more or less oppressed, both of which are unproductive for collective liberation. In this chapter, I introduce intersectionality and provide portraits with interviews that help the reader understand intersectionality from multiple lenses.

In order for you to teach intersectionally, you must understand the concept of *intersectionality*, coined by Dr. Kimberly Crenshaw in 1994 and described by Audre Lorde in 1981, and the Combahee River Collective in 1977. *Intersectionality* refers to the social, economic, and political ways in which identity-based systems of oppression and privilege connect, overlap, and influence one another. In a University of Wisconsin Madison Title IX training authored by Chynna Lewis, I learned that scholars Barrett (1999) and Lugones (2003) describe these identities as enmeshed rather than intersecting. When Lugones describes identities as enmeshed, she describes them as more like all of the ingredients of a mixture (like a smoothie) finally mixed together rather than completely autonomous lines coming together at a point. This concept helps us understand that these identities are not separable — people experience all of their identities at once.

For example, based on my identities, I can show up as a cisgender, heterosexual, first-generation, middle class Filipino American, and the list goes on. Being aware of my multiple intersecting identities helps me understand the level of power and privilege I have or don't have walking into different spaces. If my salient identities are present with the people in the space I enter, then I *may* have more power and privilege in that same space. When I visit the teachers that I work with in New York City through NYC Men Teach Asian American Teaching, Empowerment, and Development initiative (AATEND), I walk in with more power and privilege than I would if I walked into a space of non–Asian American men because most of my participants share my racial, socio-economic, and gender identities. It's not like I don't think about our differences because we all have them in this space, but since our salient identities are so similar, it's easier to notice our similarities and experiences associated with them. That's a rare example when Asian Americans get to be in coalition with other Asian Americans in education.

Asian Americans don't get the benefit of intersectionality. They are often seen as singularly Chinese. Even Chinese people are seen as all the same. I know this because I've been referred to with the terms: "Ching Chong Ching Chong," which is an outdated racist term that refers to Asians as being mistaken as Chinese. A book by Henry Carrington Bolton from 1886 — *The Counting-Out Rhymes of Children* — tersely describes this rhyme:

> *"Under the influence of Chinese cheap labor on the Pacific coast, this rhyme is improved by boys brought up to believe the 'Chinese must go,' and the result is as follows: —*
>
> *Ching, Chong, Chineeman,*
>
> *How do you sell your fish?*
>
> *Ching, Chong, Chineeman,*
>
> *Six bits a dish.*
>
> *Ching, Chong, Chineeman,*
>
> *Oh! that is too dear!*
>
> *Ching, Chong, Chineeman,*
>
> *Clear right out of here."*

While this points to some of the origins of the homogenizing term, it is also important to note that people with enormous influence and platforms, like Donald Trump, Rosie O'Donnell, and Shaquille O'Neal, have also used this term to either mock or perpetuate the perpetual foreigner stereotype toward Asian Americans.

This has happened to me as a teacher, as an instructional coach, and as a normal person just walking down the street. As an Asian American, I have trained myself not to let my triggers manifest in harmful ways, especially as an educator. We never know when students will say or do something that mocks Asian Americans, especially when the topic is presented in front of you. Lastly, I would be lying if I said this only happens to me. Being homogenized or erased from curricula because of the Black and white binary of education is something that any Asian American experiences throughout their PreK–12 tenure.

Teaching us intersectionally is a way to combat the monolithic narrative that comes out of the Black and white binary. Furthermore, it is a way to teach students how to be identity-conscious, empathetic, and how to become stronger allies toward Asian Americans.

Praxis: Action and Reflection

One way to teach Asian Americans intersectionally is to learn about Asian Americans who represent a variety of identities and then share this with your students. This is a part of helping combat Asian American erasure while painting a fuller picture of the Asian American diaspora. The following are some activities you can engage in for yourself, your class, and your school to strengthen your knowledge of intersectionality and Asian America.

Activity 1: Which Asian American Leaders Do You Know?

Returning to my opening self-assessment from Chapter 1, I want you to think about the first five Asian American leaders that come to mind when you encounter the term "Asian American." Who did you think of?

If these leaders identify ethnically as Japanese, Korean, or Chinese, then you have been socialized to automatically associate the terms "leader" and "Asian Americans" with East Asians. If these leaders are only heteronormative men, then you have been socialized to automatically associate the terms "leader" and "Asian Americans" with patriarchal standards. If these leaders only represent STEM fields, then you have been socialized to associate the terms "leader" and Asian Americans" with the trope of being seen as "science or math wiz kids." You get the picture.

Because stereotypes are so strong, to combat them, we have to actively search for other identity markers as they relate to Asian

Americans. That's the practice. The following are a few portraits of the "Asian Americans Avengers" that share an array of intersecting identities. I say "Asian American Avengers" because these leaders are educators and activists fighting for a socially just world for Asian Americans. In each portrait, I asked them a series of questions that speak to what identities matter most to them, which intersectionalities they feel most and when, and what educators should pay attention to with regard to intersectionalities and Asian Americans.

MEET TAKERU "TK" NAGAYOSHI (HE/HIM)

Question: Who are you, and what identities are important to you?

I'm an educator, son of Japanese immigrants, and gay person of color. Having grown up both in Japan and the United States, I am also bilingual and bicultural.

What identities are important depend on the context. For example, who I'm with, whether I'm navigating predominantly white institutions (PWIs), or whether being gay will be embraced, all factor in how I present and how strongly I'm able to lean into certain aspects of my identity.

In professional spaces, I navigate as "TK" instead of the Japanese name my parents gave me, Takeru. TK leans into my cultural experiences and first-generation American upbringing in the United States. But it's also easier for my colleagues to process. Takeru doesn't roll off their tongue quite

(Continues)

(Continued)

as smoothly; he's foreign and tempting to mangle. People preempt me that they'll butcher it. They'll ask that I repeat it twice, struggle through it awkwardly, and will never repeat it again because it's embarrassing to ask thrice. But TK, he's familiar and easy to remember. He's someone you'd like to reference in meetings, shout out in calls — an easily digestible name that'll never hold up the line at Starbucks because the barista always knows how to spell it. But he's not the Japanese me.

I share this code-switching experience because even in our names, it reflects how identity is contextual. People of color and those grappling with multiple intersectional identities must, depending on the context, pick and choose how to represent themselves should they desire mainstream success and acceptance (or experience life with minimal friction). What is often subsumed are those identities with relatively less privilege and power.

I'm conflicted about how to navigate as TK in professional spaces, but it works for now. But even as TK, it's important that people hear and learn my full name first. This is why I always introduce myself as Takeru "TK" Nagayoshi. Even when we choose to highlight certain parts of our identities, all of them (and their power) are always with us.

MEET ROHAN ZHOU-LEE (THEY/SIYA/祂(TĀ))

Question: Who are you, and what identities are important to you?

I am Rohan, gender identity Firebird. My Black/African, Asian, and Queer writer, trumpeter, dancer, and community organizer. Each of these are equally important to my identity, personal and inherited history and joy. My education identity is also important, surprisingly. I hold a BA in ethnomusicology, a field of musical ethnography that has historically colonial and racist roots. It is a field through which I have been able to conduct lots of research on my identity through the politics of music.

Question: Are there multiple identities that you feel at the same time? If so, how are they felt or expressed?

All of my identities are felt and experienced simultaneously. They are expressed to different degrees when it comes to code-switching. Mixed folk are especially good at this, even if we don't pass as a certain race. When at a public event, I do find myself hyper-visibilizing my mixed identity through clothing and movement. My mannerisms change, depending on the space and the cultural code of conduct. This is something I've developed a sense of thanks to my ethnomusicology degree, which to me especially informs cultural precision when entering a space. One must also know the history and cultural nuances gleaned from it. This knowledge is critical to my experience intersecting Sole Yu's concept of political imagination.

Question: For educators, do you have any advice on how to stretch their knowledge of Asian American identities and intersectionalities?

Like any other intersecting identity, nothing can be extracted from the entire experience. One cannot, for example, simply analyze Mando-pop music without its socio-political context and history. Stretching knowledge includes even the tiniest of details, because they all contribute to cultural identity, expression, and political movement. Examine any political issue, and then look up Asian American history related to it.

MEET MISO KWAK (SHE/HER)

(Continues)

(Continued)

Question: Who are you, and what identities are important to you?

First and foremost, I am Miso. Growing up in South Korea, I liked my name from a young age, because people often complimented how pretty my name is. In Korean, "miso" means smile.

When I came to the US with my family as a teenager, I briefly went through a time when I wanted to have a different name for my new teachers and classmates in America, because so many of them mispronounced my name and/or asked me if I am Japanese. Many people still do, but as I have come to embrace my existence and identity as a Korean-American, I am glad that I kept my name instead of adopting a name that would let me blend in more seamlessly to American life. I am proud to be a Korean-American, and thankful that identifying as a Korean-American gives me access to the diverse AAPI community more broadly.

I am also proud to be a member of the disability community. Specifically, I am blind. I have been blind as long as I can remember, but my critical consciousness around my lived experience as a blind person and a member of the disability community at large began to develop during my undergraduate years when I had an opportunity to learn about the resilient and fearless disabled activists who came before me for the first time. Now I strive to contribute to and continue building this rich community.

These two identities — being a Korean-American and being a blind person — are the two most salient identities for me because as much as I hold pride in these identities, I also have to constantly think about how to negotiate these identities as I navigate the world that does not readily value either of these identity markers. My vigilance was especially high when I went to cast my vote in the recent election. Will someone question my US citizenship status? Will there be an accessible voting machine and will the poll workers know how to set it up? What should I say if anyone expresses any doubt on my capability and right to vote?

The mental energy it takes to think about the various forms of microaggression and systemic barriers I may face, how to negotiate them, and how to decide which ones are worth my energy to fight back — all of these can be tiresome and difficult.

Nonetheless, being a Korean-American and a disabled person — these are the cornerstone of who I am. My life experiences shaped by these identities motivate me to be an explorer and a bridge-builder. My intersecting identities teach me not to limit myself in my understanding of others, in imagination of what our world could be, and in aspiration of who I can become. Similarly, my intersecting identities encourage me to build bridges — between the AAPI community and disability, between university campuses, legislatures, and classrooms, and between the various academic disciplines.

Question: Are there multiple identities that you feel at the same time? If so, how are they felt?

Even before I learned the term "intersectionality," I knew that I am both a Korean American and a blind person. I cannot pinpoint exactly where the two identities separate because they are all intertwined. These identities are not like a scarf or hat I can choose to wear or not wear based on my mood or the weather. I have to wear both identities every day and all day.

How and to what extent I feel them, however, largely depend on where I am and whom I am surrounded by. For a long time, I had a hard time feeling a true sense of belonging in the Korean American or AAPI spaces. Although I cherished the shared experiences I had growing up in an Asian immigrant household, too often, I had to advocate for greater accessibility for me to feel fully included as a blind person. For example, when I go to picnics of a sort organized by Korean American or AAPI groups, I anticipate activities that are most likely not accessible for me. The lack of forethought on accessibility is not just an AAPI community problem, but it is still worth pointing out.

The story is not that much different in reverse. In the spaces that primarily focus on disabled people, I have felt misunderstood or not understood at all many times when it came to my experiences as an Asian American immigrant. For example, nearly every major disability rights activist I learned about in college was white. On a more systemic level, I couldn't access certain benefits or opportunities that my disabled peers had because of my immigration status, and I didn't quite know where would be the space in which I could process such experience safely and comfortably.

In either case, I have this feeling, knowing that I am a minority. I think it is in part because of the actually small number of people who are both Asian and disabled. More importantly, however, there is not enough space yet that fosters an environment that encourages expression and embracing of both of these identities simultaneously.

Question: For educators, do you have any advice on how to stretch their knowledge of Asian American identities and intersectionalities?

Think about the diversity from the beginning. When students are learning about the AAPI community, are they being exposed to stories that go beyond that of the East Asians? Are they getting an opportunity to learn about Asian Americans who are also part of other cultural communities, such as the LGBTQ+ community, disability community, and different religious

(Continues)

(Continued)

communities? Whose voices are missing in the curriculum? Considerations on diverse, intersectional representation cannot be an afterthought. Challenge the dominant norm and dig deeper, and encourage your colleagues and students to do the same.

Going hand in hand, another important thing would be to foster a space in which students feel comfortable exploring and expressing their identities. Acknowledging that identities can be complex and that identities evolve over time would be the first step. With this in mind, some of the concrete steps that educators can take are: 1) inviting guest speakers who hold diverse intersectional identities who can speak about their own journey, 2) honoring and celebrating students' multilingual and multicultural backgrounds (e.g., asking students to share their favorite poems or folktales they heard from their parents, in their home language if desired), and 3) engaging in creative exercises that encourage students to explore and express their identities (e.g., storytelling or artistic expressions).

MEET SHYAM GADWAL (HE/HIM)

Question: Who are you, and what identities are important to you?

I'm a child of the 80s, when reading books earned me free pizza and finding coupons for fried chicken meant a wonderful night. My parents immigrated from Hyderabad, India (ancestral land), and I was born in Baltimore, Maryland, United States (colonized land) making me Indian-American.

And that's how I saw it, Indian-and-American. Gratitude for my first teachers (parents) for instilling pride that my Indian ancestors were from cultures and histories that thrived for thousands of years. Belief in my parent's immigrant sacrifice, to grow up disconnected from our extended family (grandparents, cousins, mummy's sisters, papa's best friends), so that we could have an excellent American education.

My education wasn't excellent, it was sufficient though. After federal courts decided my public school system didn't adequately desegregate, the county was forced into creating a bussing and magnet school strategy to achieve racial balance. It didn't work.

Despite traveling an hour to attend a STEM school, I was one of a handful of non-Black students in majority Black schools. We were insulated to be ourselves as students and affirmed by our educators from a white dominant world. And while I benefited from this nurturing environment as a student of color, I never felt like I could reciprocate with my identity.

The distance away from school made being Indian safe from being American. My classmates were unaware and unable to ostracize my aromatic meals, colorful clothes, and Dravidian language. As the oldest child, I wrote the first draft of being Indian-and-American for my parents, my sisters, and myself.

Question: Are there multiple identities that you feel at the same time? If so, how are they felt?

As a first-generation college student, each year pursuing my science degree became progressively stressful. Not only was the subject more difficult, but I was out of place. I lived on campus and traveled to both coasts for internships. I spent more time at school than at home. Keeping my academic challenges away from my family meant I agreed to keep myself away from my strongest support system.

I further dug into this arrangement with new, unhealthy diet habits. Eventually, culminating in a diabetes diagnosis my senior year of college. What was hereditarily predisposed was accelerated in this new socialpolitical environment.

Diabetes did not offer any distance to transverse either my Indian-and-American identity. It was a part of me that both sides would need to reconcile my new body as I participated in meal-centric activities. Coffee interviews. First dates. Mithai boxes. Conference buffets. Prasadum blessings. Bottomless brunches.

Though I wondered, what would my body would sacrifice to avoid offending an auntie's biryani or a colleague's round of drinks?

My diabetes is part of who I am just like my Indian American identity. It shows up in different places, some more comfortable and safe to navigate than others.

(Continues)

(Continued)

Question: For educators, do you have any advice on how to stretch their knowledge of Asian American identities and intersectionalities?

The power of teaching about the Asian American experience through an intersectional lens is that educators humanize our community. We all have the opportunity to learn through the compassion of our similarities and the appreciation of our differences. Stories are within all of us and are worth sharing. In this act of allyship, everyone benefits.

MEET ANDREA KIM (SHE/HER)

Question: Who are you, and what identities are important to you?

My name is Andrea Kim Neighbors, and I identify as a mixed-race Korean and white cisgender woman. I've always identified strongly as mixed-race, my parents always made sure that my brother and I understood that we come from different cultures, and they can teach us many things about who we are and who we can be. I grew up as a navy brat, so we moved many times.

I say I grew up in both San Diego, California, and Yokosuka, Japan. I was born in Honolulu, Hawaii, but I have no memories of living there as a child. In California and Japan, I grew up with Korean, Mexican, Filipino, and Japanese friends, aunties and uncles. My immediate community, which was almost always comprised of peers and their parents through life on and around a military base, was predominantly Asian and mixed-race. Seeing others that looked like me and my mom was very normal, and looking back, I see how special and important that was.

In elementary school, I learned I was different at a very young age by my teachers, who sometimes made decisions on who I am and how I identify. I've always been a three-name person. My middle name, Kim, was my mom's maiden name and it was passed down to me. When I was in elementary school a teacher insisted that Kim was short for the name Kimberly, which was very frustrating for me. Another teacher had insisted my hair was brown, not black. I remember these moments clearly as an adult, early memories of when I learned that not everyone would believe me when I say I am mixed, and instead, decide for me who I am and who I must be.

Question: Are there multiple identities that you feel at the same time? If so, how are they felt?

I've always identified as mixed-race but I have more affinity with my Korean heritage. I've never identified as white, even though I know I'm sometimes viewed as fully white or just racially ambiguous, when people can't "figure me out." There's a lot of confusion that comes with this experience, along with a lot of pain, guilt and the desire to minimize myself as much as possible.

No matter where I go, I feel grounded in my identity, but how others view me will always be different. I hold many privileges as a white and East Asian able-bodied person, and it has allowed me to navigate different parts of the world with little to no issue. When I lived in Alaska, I was seen as a member of the Aleut culture. In the Russian Far East, during my graduate fieldwork, I passed as a local Asian and Russian person, or just Korean, to my surprise by white Russians. In Northern Europe, I was seen as Finnish. I would correct people every time, explaining my background, which sometimes led to others expressing disappointment, as if I was more acceptable living as their assumption. It's a strange experience to be seen as something you do not identify with, unquestionably so. In my experiences of passing, I feel as if I move in some parts of the world with an invisible cloak, never seen, but always floating in the background.

Question: For educators, do you have any advice on how to stretch their knowledge of Asian American identities and intersectionalities?

I would advise educators to think about who they include when they hear "Asian American." Asian Americans are mixed white, Black, Latinx, Native American. Asian Americans can also identify with different racial and ethnic groups, abilities, genders, religions. With one's many identities, there are also many stories and ways of expressing one's truth. Honor a student's name and the stories behind it, and what it means to them. Honor how

(Continues)

(Continued)

students express their cultures, languages, foods, faiths, without tokenizing or making them feel different. Ask students if they are open to collaborating with you and peers about how they can share their cultures as a classroom community.

Also understand that students may not feel comfortable or safe sharing their stories with you and their peers — they don't owe anyone their truth. There is a lot that educators can learn about Asian American identities and intersectionalities by looking to who is living in their community. Strike up a conversation with someone in the Asian American community and get to know them as human beings — ask them about their day, what they are looking forward to, how their family is, and let the conversation grow. In my experience moving around the world, and having to learn how to meet new people on my own, I've never taken for granted the moments I've shared with complete strangers, former neighbors and classmates, store owners, etc. You can learn a lot about identities and intersectionalities just by listening and a willingness to be open.

Activity 2: Gallery Walk to Activate Background Knowledge or Schema

One way you can start the conversation around Asian Americans and intersectionality is having a gallery walk of these Asian American Avengers and interviews. There are so many ways you can incorporate a gallery walk, but I will focus on activating background knowledge or schema so students can create a relationship with the narratives. For those who have not conducted a gallery walk, here are a few instructions:

1. Print out the image and the interview of each Asian American Avenger.

2. Post them throughout the room.

3. Set an intention for students to read and learn from each Asian American Avenger. When I say intention, this can be a question around identity and intersections and how they connect with each leader. My example questions for activating background knowledge are:

   a. Which Asian American Avenger narratives resonated with you? Why?

   b. Which Asian American Avenger narratives challenged you? Why?

4. Give students about 20–30 minutes to engage in the entire walk. This allows kids processing time to meet each Avenger and read their interviews.

Activity 3: Living Portraits and Perspective-Taking

To push the gallery walk activity further, I've added the concept of a "living portrait" to keep these images on the wall *all year long* and refer to what type of perspective this person could give when encountering new topics throughout the class. As a teacher I would do this with different leaders who represent different identities and walks of life that allow for perspective-taking to always live in your classroom. When talking about the model minority myth, you can stop the class and post one of the following questions:

◆ How would Rohan respond to this situation similarly or differently from Miso?

◆ How could a Brown Asian perspective interpret this issue in [insert text]?

◆ How would a multi-racial or mixed-race perspective interpret [insert character's actions] from [insert text chapter]? What would Andrea Kim or Rohan Zhou-Lee do differently in the same scenario?

This enables students to revisit narratives, which allows for students to normalize and solidify these images in their brains. This reflection question also aligns with practicing the skill of comparing and contrasting differing perspectives.

Activity 4: Perspective-Taking with Another Text That Has Similar Racialized Themes

When teaching seventh grade, I had the opportunity to co-develop a curriculum around the famous memoir *When I was Puerto Rican* by Esmeralda Santiago. This memoir entails a young Puerto Rican girl, Negi, exploring the American Dream through immigrating from Puerto Rico to New York, and the joy and struggle that come along with immigration stories. The following is a brief lesson plan structure of how I thought about Chapter 8 of this book and how we can intentionally refer to the "Asian American Avengers."

Chapter & Pages	Objective	Key Questions	How to Refer back to Asian American Avengers
Chapter 8 Pages 65–76	Students will: Identify and explain the author's perspective on American colonialism. Identify and explain the effects of American colonialism in Puerto Rico.	• Why do Americans come to Macún? • What do the Americans try to teach the women? • What are the cultural problems with the charts and information? (pages 66–67) • What is significant about el purgante on page 69? • How do the people in the community characterize the US?	• What perspective do you think the Asian American Avenger has on American colonialism? • What perspective do you think the Asian American Avenger thinks about how the Americans teach the women in this chapter? • How do concepts of gender intersect some of the narratives of the Asian American Avenger and that of Negi?

Activity 5: Perspective-Taking with a Text That Does Not Have Racialized Themes

Outside of concepts that are usually and explicitly attributed to Asian Americans like the model minority myth or the perpetual foreigner stereotype, being able to reflect on what Asian Americans think about a totally different topic can help normalize whose perspective we center or value when it comes to perspective-taking in general. It challenges our students' biases on who has the jurisdiction over which topics and why.

So yes, I want teachers to refer to the Asian American Avengers, especially when texts are not explicitly connected to an Asian American political story. The following is an example of a lesson plan structure I co-developed with the play *Death of a Salesman* by Arthur Miller. This play is another classic that is taught in middle schools and high schools across the United States. It is a critique on labor, capitalism, and the American Dream.

CHAPTER & PAGES	OBJECTIVE	KEY QUESTIONS	HOW TO REFER BACK TO ASIAN AMERICAN AVENGERS
Chapter 7 Pages 52–62	Students will: Identify how capitalism manifests with the interaction between Willy and his supervisor. Identify how capitalism plays a role in the book as a whole.	• On page 61, what does Willy mean by "You can't eat the orange and throw the peel away"? What does it reveal about Miller's views on American culture (capitalism)? • p. 61 What does it mean to Willy to die a "Death of a Salesman"?	• What perspective do you think the Asian American Avenger has on capitalism and labor? • Assign different Asian American Avengers to each student in your class and ask how they think that particular Asian American Avenger would describe the American Dream.

In *When I was Puerto Rican*, the connection between a colonized narrative has strong potential for students to learn how similar colonization looks between different ethnoracial groups. There is a missed opportunity when we do not talk about the enmeshed narratives that can potentially lead to solidarity between different systematically marginalized groups. I talk about this more in Chapter 6. When it comes to referring back to the Asian American Avengers' perspective toward Arthur Miller's *Death of a Salesman*, this normalizes that our perspective is valuable and legible across literature genres.

A Movement, Not a Moment

Teaching about Asian American representation and the intersections of our identity is best when they appear in our lives every single day. One of the best ways of ensuring that you, your students, and your school learn about Asian American perspectives all year long is to have resources ready to refer to. The following is a list of resources that help teach about intersectionality and Asian Americans:

TITLE/LINK	AUTHOR(S)	WHAT'S IN THIS RESOURCE?
Toolkit for Teaching at the Intersections www.learningforjustice.org/ magazine/summer-2016/ toolkit-for-teaching-at-the-intersections	Learning for Justice, Issue 53, Summer 2016	This resource offers a lesson plan on teaching the concept of intersectionality through an anti-bias framework. This link also connects readers to their anti-bias teaching standards.
Why We Turn to Intersectionality to Confront Anti-Asian Violence ncg.org/news/ why-we-turn-intersectionality-confront-anti-asian-violence	Alice Y. Hom, Equity, the Social Justice Director at Northern California Grant-makers (NCG).	This resource offers perspective and education on why we must see anti-Asian violence as connected to the interlocking identities of sexism, heterosexism, racism, classism, and more.
We Want to Be Intersectional: Asian American College Students Extracurricular Rhetorical Education cfshrc.org/article/we-want-to-be-intersectional-asian-american-college-students-extracurricular-rhetorical-education/	Allison Dziuba, Vol 23, Issue 4 of *Coalition of Feminist Scholars in the History of Rhetoric and Composition*	This resource explores three Asian American college student groups creating spaces of intellectual and social belonging through their longing to be intersectional. The emphasis on this research highlights the extracurricular nature of exploring and leveraging intersectionality as a theoretical and discursive framework.
Queer and Asian Identities www.youtube.com/ watch?v=Ko4V3X4Qc70	Soukprida Phetmisy and Takeru Nagayoshi in The Smithsonian Asian Pacific American Center	This resource explores two Asian American queer-identifying educators discussing the intersection of being queer, Asian, and Queer-Asian.

Chapter 6

Isang Bagsak as an Educational Framework

LEARNING OBJECTIVES:

♦ Participants will understand the historical context around the concept of Isang Bagsak (knowledge).

♦ Participants will stretch their definition of Isang Bagsak to understand this as an educational framework (knowledge and mindset).

♦ Participants will learn about and how to teach moments in history that involve Asian Americans in a cross-racial movement (knowledge and skill).

The Personal Is Political

Isang Bagsak as Verb
In Tagalog translated as
Unity as verb
Unity as action
across lines of difference
across lines of passion

This mini poem is part of a longer poem that I wrote during the rise of anti-Asian hate in 2020. Isang Bagsak [ee-sung, bugsak] is a noun and ontology. As described in the ethnic studies model curriculum published in 2022 by the California Department of Education, Isang Bagsak translates to "one down" and is adopted from a ritual used by Anti-Martial Law activists in the Philippines. To show solidarity, Isang Bagsak was powerfully proclaimed by a member of the Anti-Martial Law movement in the 1970s, and in unison the community would make a loud sound either by clapping or stomping.

Over time, many activists and movement builders have borrowed Isang Bagsak to show unity at their marches, protests, meetings, and events. Artnelson Concordia, a teacher-activist and scholar, and two other Filipino American organizers involved with the Philippine Peasant Support Network (PESANTE), combined Isang Bagsak with the United Farm Workers' Unit Clap in the early 1990s. The combination of the Unity Clap and Isang Bagsak starts off with a slow clap and crescendos in a faster pace clap that culminates in someone yelling "ISANG BAGSAK." The community responds with a single clap or stomp symbolizing cross-racial solidarity.

I remember when I first experienced Isang Bagsak. It was in an Asian American education affinity space. Justin Tandingan, a fellow Filipino American educator and leader, summoned Isang Bagsak by having all one hundred of us circle up and participate in the ritual. It was somatic, and till this day that feeling of unity still lives in my body. From that moment, I started summoning Isang Bagsak in almost every organizing convening I led, which pushed me to question: *What if this was more than just a ritual?* Beyond culture as a symbol, American sociologist Dr. Ann Swidler defines "culture' as a toolkit of symbols, rituals, stories, worldviews, which people can use in varying configurations to solve problems."

Applying this sociological lens, I started to see Isang Bagsak in other expansions. One of these expansions is with Dr. Minju Bae who wrote about Isang Bagsak as a tool to analyze Asian and Asian American racial formation and organizing in the 1980s. Another activist-scholar, Dr. Allyson Tintiangco-Cubales, curated events that centered Isang Bagsak as a tool to scale cross-racial Filipino American and Black solidarity. Tintiangco-Cubales extended Isang Bagsak as a tool to help organizers and scholars think about collective solidarity in a temporal way. She expanded Isang Bagsak into Dalawang Bagsak (two down) and Tatlong Bagsak (three down), a symbol that speaks to our past, present, and future. For me, I'm broadening the term to mean an educational framework that challenges education actors in the following ways:

◆ Combating the Black-white binary by teaching cross-racial movements

◆ Shift student and staff mindsets from scarcity to abundance

◆ Embrace multi-partial facilitation

The ultimate goal of this chapter is to further expand the cultural concept of Isang Bagsak into an educational framework, which requires an understanding of how it can be applied in praxis. In translating Filipino rituals into tangible practice, I'm engaging in radical imagination. I'm stretching the imagination because for too long cultural concepts from people of color have been omitted, undervalued, or appropriated.

The Praxis: Action and Reflection

When I refer to praxis, I start with the Brazilian philosopher Paulo Freire's 1972 concept of praxis: "Reflection and action upon the world in order to transform it." But for Isang Bagsak to serve as an anti-racist tool, we must briefly visit Eric Yamamoto's concept of Critical Race Praxis (CRP). Although he grounds CRP in the case of law and critical race theory, Yamamoto's overall conclusions on bridging theory to community and groundwork is salient to the development of Isang Bagsak as an educational framework. In order for Isang Bagsak as an educational framework to be effective, we must see it in the lens of CRP.

Furthermore, my version of cross-racial solidarity is different from normative versions of "interracial praxis," which is an outcome of Yamamoto's work. Isang Bagsak as an educational framework is about cross-racial solidarity, but it forces the education actor using the framework to include Asian Americans in this narrative to combat the omission of Asian Americans from social justice work.

This chapter is part of a movement of molding theory into practice again, from culture and symbolism into educational framework that leaves participants with something they can do with their education organizations. Below are a few ways to concretize Isang Bagsak as an educational framework with a reflection question to reinforce the concept of praxis.

Combating the Black-White Binary by Teaching Cross-Ethnoracial Movements

Isang Bagsak as an educational framework charges education actors to build their knowledge of cross-ethnoracial movements specifically involving Asian Americans. Within white supremacy logic, the Black-white binary truncates history by attempting to teach civil rights progress in a linear fashion, which omits Asian Americans and other people of color (Perea, 1997). For example, when we talk about critical race theory (CRT), most contemporary articles do not mention one of its founding theorists, Mari Matsuda, a Japanese American lawyer, activist, and law professor at the University of Hawaii. When we talk about the fight for labor rights during the Delano Grape Strike, people often champion Cesar Chavez without any mention of the Filipinos that started the movement. When we talk about racism and oppression, we rarely talk about Asian Americans because people have this idea that Asian Americans never experience racial oppression due to the model minority myth. Learning about and bringing cross-racial movements into an organization as a core educational framework can disrupt the Black-white binary that is taught, learned, and perpetuated both in and outside educational organizations.

Within this component of Isang Bagsak as an educational framework, one explicit example is to include and teach cross-racial movements including Asian Americans in your school's curriculum. Focusing on Black, Blasian, and Asian American solidarity, the following are historical moments (past and present) that embody Isang Bagsak: the Buffalo Soldiers, The Black Feminist Writing Movement, Bengali Harlem, the Fight for Ethnic Studies, and The Blasian March.

CORPORAL DAVID FAGEN, THE BUFFALO SOLDIERS, AND THE BLACK FEMINIST WRITING MOVEMENT (1899–1902):

Corporal David Fagen of the 24th Infantry of the Buffalo Soldiers was openly against the harsh treatment of Filipinos from White US troops during the Philippine American War. The White US troops would refer to Filipinos with the term "N-Word." Corporal David Fagen accepted a commission as an officer in the rebel army and fought against the American forces for two years. He fought in the Brigade of General Urbano Lacuna in central Luzon. While originally commissioned as a lieutenant, Fagen's valor, guile, and many military successes led to his promotion to the rank of captain. Because he was a successful guerilla leader, the American military became obsessed with his capture. His exploits were reported in the *Manila Times*, and in several American newspapers.

While Corporal David Fagen of the Buffalo Soldiers exhibited Isang Bagsak overseas, Isang Bagsak was happening from writers and journalists such as Ida B. Wells, Anna Julia Cooper, and the Black Feminist Movement who openly wrote and spoke out against the Philippine American War (Figure 6.1).

BENGALI MUSLIMS (1920S–1960S)

From reading excerpts from *Bengali Harlem* and research from Professor Vivek Bald at MIT, one omitted Isang Bagsak story that I realized I did not know enough about is Bengali Muslims. According to Bald, in the 1920s–1930s, South Asian seamen would jump British ships and live in eastern and northern cities, including Baltimore, Detroit, and New York City. In the process, many Bengalis, who lived in close proximity to African-Americans and Puerto Ricans, found themselves marrying into those communities.

Bengali Harlem of the 1950s–1960s was a time when Bengali and other South Asian immigrants settled in Harlem. The cross-racial affinity went both ways as you saw African American leaders such as Malcolm X and Miles Davis frequent Bengali Harlem. Malcolm X would debate the tenets of Islam with Bengali friends. Miles Davis was also known to be going over Bollywood tracks while in Harlem.

FIGURE 6.1   Anna Julia Cooper (left) and Ida B. Wells (right)

FIGURE 6.2 "No History No Self" sign

THE FIGHT FOR ETHNIC STUDIES (1969)

Beyond labor rights and military solidarity movements, Isang Bagsak happened with the inaugural formation of Ethnic Studies at San Francisco State College. From November 1968 through March 1969, the Third World Liberation Front (TWLF) held the longest student-led strike in US history (see Figure 6.2).

TWLF was a cross-coalition between the Black Student Union (BSU), the Latin American Student Organization (LASO), the Mexican American Student Coalition (MASC), the Pilipino American Collegiate Endeavor (PACE), the Asian American Political Alliance (AAPA), and the Intercollegiate Chinese for Social Action (ICSA) group. The purpose was to ensure that students saw themselves in the college curriculum and in leadership. Leaders Pat Salavar and Ron Quidachay aimed to strengthen Filipino socio-political consciousness, especially regarding racism and colonialism. Ron served as the chairman of the TWLF a year before the strike, which speaks to the influence that Asian Americans, specifically Filipino Americans, had on this movement.

BLASIAN MARCH (2020–PRESENT)

Cycling back to the chapter on intersectionality and Asian American Avengers, I want to bring back the work of Rohan Zhou-Lee, They/Siya/祂 (Tā), founder of the Blasian March. The Blasian March is a present day solidarity action through education and mutual celebration between Black/African, Asian, and mixed Blasian communities (see Figure 6.3).

The first Blasian March took place on October 11, 2020, in New York City. All speakers were women, LGBT, or disabled, including a written statement from organizers currently residing in Palestine. Protestors used music and dancing to build solidarity with chants such as "Black Lives Matter," "Asians 4 Black Lives," and "Black Power, Asian Power." This action marked the six-year anniversary of the murder of trans Filipina woman Jennifer Laude by US marine Michael Pemberton. Protesters in New York City honored her by chanting "Justice for Jennifer." Beyond the formal march, the Blasian March team organizes an annual book fair of all ages and genres that centers on Black, Asian, and Blasian writers.

REFLECTION QUESTIONS

What are other moments in history (past, present) where we see Asian Americans involved with other social movements? What was their role?

FIGURE 6.3 Blasian March

Photographer: Sameasy Shoots

Shift Staff and Student Mindsets from Scarcity to Abundance

Beyond cross-racial coalitions, there are a few concepts that Isang Bagsak can help reinforce when thinking about cross-group collaborations. The first concept that Isang Bagsak reinforces is the concept of scarcity mindset versus abundance mindset. Having a scarcity mindset basically means that there are limited resources, therefore possibility is stifled. Having an abundance mindset means the opposite as you can see in the following table.

SCARCITY	ABUNDANCE
Not enough resources to share	More than enough resources to share
I hold all the knowledge	Willingness to learn from others
Reluctant to collaborate	Willingness to collaborate
Amplifies one's own accomplishments	Amplifies the accomplishments of themselves and others
Fixed mindset	Fluid and open mindset

When school clubs or affinity resource groups get their funding allocations for the year, it is easy to think through a scarcity mindset and think of all the things you cannot achieve with your budget. When planning for a school district or school's financial year, using Isang Bagsak as a lens can help you think about the possibility of combining resources or finding ways to get what you need to achieve whatever outcomes you aim for both on the front end of planning and as an adaptive measure. Combining resources helps us think of the 1965 Delano Grape Strike, where Filipino and Mexican farm workers combined resources and social and human capital to organize and fight for better labor conditions and funding.

REFLECTION QUESTIONS

Have you ever had a moment when you fell into a scarcity mindset? Could this have changed if you combined resources with another group?

Embrace Multi-Partial Facilitation

Multi-partiality means the ability to balance multiple perspectives at once but ensuring that we center the narratives of historically and systematically marginalized communities per respective topic. I learned about this in 2019 while I was on a panel centering Asian Americans in Miami called "Let's Ask an Asian American." A white male was excited to share their perspective on this topic because he had Asian American family members and he'd been to Asia. So he decided to interject during the panel to give his opinions and perspectives after each question was posed to the panel.

The downside of this is that whiteness was centered in a space meant to center Asian Americans. On top of that Asian Americans rarely get the time to be in coalition with each other in Miami, which made this even worse. Of course, I fault the white man for sharing his ideas, but at the same time, the moderator did not address this person right away, which permitted him to continue. You're probably wondering what this has to do with Asian American perspectives and teaching. Here's how I think about it in three stages: designing the discussion, facilitating, and participating:

When designing:

◆ How are you thinking about the social emotional needs of your audience?

◆ How are you thinking about the accessibility needs of your audience?

When facilitating:

◆ Name and notice patterns of participation based on identities and proximity to the issue at hand.

◆ Pause the flow of dialogue to softly invite different voices in a discussion, especially if the group having the discussion has a strong homogenous identifier.

When participating:

◆ If you feel as if you missed your opportunity to participate/speak/share an idea, stop the flow and share this.

◆ If you feel you are taking up a lot of airtime, step back to listen and acknowledge this so others are metacognitive about the intentional shift.

> **REFLECTION QUESTIONS**
>
> What does Isang Bagsak mean to you after reading this chapter?
>
> What ways do you imagine using Isang Bagsak in your classroom or school?

A Movement, Not a Moment

Today, more than ever, we need the power of Isang Bagsak in a reductionist era of conservative pundits and politics promoting anti-CRT, anti-wokeness, anti–political education, and basically anti-truth. Teaching the truth is vital in preserving democracy within our schools. Isang Bagsak as an educational framework combats the Black-white binary that omits Asian Americans from conversations and spaces of racial justice, and ensures that we tell the truth about their contributions. Isang Bagsak as an educational framework helps education actors frame their programs and discussions with abundance mindsets in order to lean into expansiveness and radical imagination. Finally, Isang Bagsak as an educational framework pushes education actors to strengthen and hold a multi-partial lens while leading their communities in social justice conversations. Beyond practical application of Isang Bagsak, simply knowing Isang Bagsak as an educational framework also validates how Filipino culture can be used as a valid, nuanced, and reputable tool in disrupting white supremacy culture.

The following are a few resources that highlight both an inter- and intra-Asian American education centering on cross-ethnoracial solidarity.

TITLE/LINK	AUTHOR(S)	WHAT'S IN THIS RESOURCE?
Isang Bagsak As Verb: Combating Anti-Blackness in Education tinyurl.com/ isangbagsakasverb	Tony DelaRosa in AAPI Alliances at Teach for America and Disruptive Partners	This resource includes a virtual panel of education practitioners and scholars that identify as Black, BlackaPina, and Filipino. It includes a graphic tool created by Rubilly Wilson for reference.

TITLE/LINK	AUTHOR(S)	WHAT'S IN THIS RESOURCE?
Asian Latinx History is Latin American History, So Why Are They Left Out? www.popsugar.com/smart-living/asian-latinx-history-is-latin-american-history-48847416	Yvette Montoya	This resource explores why Asian Latines are removed and gate-kept from Latin American history. Montoya includes Los Chinos Indios, the Mexican revolution, and its impact on Chinese workers and Mexican women.
The Brown Asian American Movement: Advocating for South Asian, Southeast Asian, and Filipino American Communities aapr.hkspublications .org/2020/02/02/the-brown-asian-american-movement-advocating-for-south-asian-southeast-asian-and-filipino-american-communities/	Kevin Nadal, PhD in the Asian American Policy Review at Harvard	This resource provides context on the Brown Asian American movement between Filipinos, South Asians, and Southeast Asian Americans. It goes over the history and offers policy recommendations to improve the lives and conditions for these communities.
Cross-Racial Solidarity Movement & The Formation of Asian American Identity www.immigranthistory.org/asamidentity.html	The Immigrant History Initiative	This resource provides lesson plans on the Civil Rights Movement, the Yellow Power Movement, and more.

Chapter 7

Colonization, War, Colonial Mentality, and Settler Colonialism

LEARNING OBJECTIVES:

◆ Practitioners will understand how Asian Americans are connected to the American tradition of colonization and war (knowledge).

◆ Practitioners will understand colonization and its impact on colonial mentality (knowledge).

◆ Practitioners will understand how Asian Americans actively partake in settler colonialism (knowledge).

◆ Practitioners will understand how to teach with a decolonial lens (skill).

The Personal Is Political

"Until we're able to acknowledge the fact that the United States is built for war, has been built for wars since the very beginning, and that Asian Americans only exist in the United States because of this kind of history, we're not going to be able to really talk about what it means to be Asian American."

—Viet Thanh Nguyen

You can't teach Asian American narratives and histories without talking about colonization, war, and the harmful residues that follow. As author Viet Thanh Nguyen asserts in an interview with the *Asian American Policy Review,* Asian American existence is inextricable from war and colonization (Huang, 2021). From war and colonization, we can understand voluntary and involuntary Asian American migration. From war and colonization, we can make sense of Asian Americans and racial triangulation, the relationship between Asian Americans, whiteness, and the Black community (Kim, 1999). We can understand Asian Americans and racial capitalism, and how we fit into the capitalist structures of America.

For this chapter, the hope is that you understand the beginnings of how to talk about colonization, war, and Asian Americans. This chapter focuses on a lot of knowledge building and reflection questions. These same reflection questions can be used with students and staff in order to help them reflect on this entrenched topic of colonization. The chapter ends with an activity to help you teach with a decolonial lens.

REFLECTION QUESTIONS

What were the earliest messages you received about Asian Americans and War? What is colonial mentality? How can you start decolonizing your teaching practice pertaining to Asian Americans?

Praxis: Action and Reflection

My first recollection of Asian Americans and war always goes back to World War II and the Vietnam War. One would think I would have a stronger recollection of various Asian American connections to war, having spent my elementary years at Mary Fay Pendleton, an elementary school on a Marine Corps base. From a formal standpoint, my teachers did not mention Asian Americans until the subject of war. From an informal education standpoint, I would learn about these two wars from documentaries shown in class or musicals like *Miss Saigon*, which centers on the story of white saviorism through a heteropatriarchal lens.

Twenty-five years later, after researching Asian American history, I learned that Asian Americans were involved in the War of 1812, the Civil War, the Spanish-American War, the Philippine American War, and World War I. The big question I keep circling back to is *why did it take 25 years for me to learn this?*

REFLECTION QUESTIONS

When was your first recollection of Asian Americans and war? Why was that the event or time period? How were they involved?

Asian Americans and Wartime Service

When it comes to painting a fuller picture of Asian Americans and war, teachers have a limited idea of how we were involved because most history texts and classes focus primarily on Japanese internment camps, the Korean American War, and the Vietnam War. Similar to my experience with informal education, movies to this day center the white male savior gaze. In addition, when Asian Americans get their 15 seconds of spotlight in formal and informal education, the lens is usually told through passive subjectivity or negative stereotyping. In reality, Asian Americans have played many different active roles in United States and Asian war relations despite having experienced exclusion, racism, and incarceration.

I offer the following stories you should read and incorporate into your history and literature classes pertaining to World War II, should they make sense. A caveat here is to know that these are not meant to glorify the military-industrial complex but rather to amplify the invisible narratives of Asian Americans who served the US.

HAZEL LEE, MAGGIE GEE, AND THE WASPs

Hazel Lee and Maggie Gee were two Chinese American women who became pilots and joined the Women Airforce Service Pilots (WASP) program in 1943. Lee and Gee were both enamored by flying. When Lee saw her first plane in 1932, she promised to get her pilot's license. Gee was a fan of Amelia Earhart. Both Lee and Gee straddled the identity crisis that comes with being an Asian American woman pilot living in an era and society influenced by racism toward Asian Americans.

Tragically, Lee died from injuries after an air collision in 1944. Gee later achieved her degree in physics at the University of California, Berkeley. The United States government did not recognize the WASP as veterans until 1977, and later, they were collectively given the Congressional Gold Medal of Honor (Figure 7.1).

FIGURE 7.1 WASP pilot

FILIPINO AMERICAN WORLD WAR II VETERANS AND HUNTER-ROTC GUERILLAS

During World War II, over 200,000 Filipino Americans fought and served the United States against the Japanese invasion (Figure 7.2). One of the largest battles that often goes untold is the Battle of Manila 1945. This battle was the second most devastating event next to Warsaw. There were over 100,000 casualties.

One notable invisible story is that of the Hunter-ROTC guerillas, which was a Philippine-US regiment. This group of around 300 cadets, led by Colonel Eleuterio Adevoso along with the United States 11th Airborne Division, fought against the Japanese to secure the University of Santo Tomas, the Malacanang Palace, and the Legislative Building housing the Philippine Congress. Similar to the WASPs, it took many years before the United States recognized Filipino American Veterans for their service. According to the Filipino Veterans Recognition and Education Project (FilVetREP), the project was formed to create a national campaign to raise awareness through academic research and public education

FIGURE 7.2   Filipino World War II veteran

and obtain national recognition of the Filipino-American World War II soldiers for their wartime service to the United States and the Philippines from July 1941 to December 1946.

Because of their organizing, on December 14, 2016, President Obama signed into law the Filipino Veterans of World War II Congressional Gold Medal Act. On October 25, 2017, Former House Speaker Paul Ryan awarded the Congressional Gold Medals to over 600 Veterans and Families.

TENSION WHILE BEING ASIAN AND GAY IN THE MILITARY

This story briefly highlights the intersectionality of being Asian American and gay in the military. Takenori "TAK" Yamamoto, a Japanese American gay activist, served in the military despite having experienced the impact of being incarcerated under President Franklin D. Roosevelt's Executive Order 9066. We have to sit with the tension and multiple levels of invisibility and oppression here. On one level, Yamamoto experienced the perpetual foreigner stereotype through forced incarceration. On another level, the intersection of being Japanese, gay, and in the United States military can also present the story of toxic masculinity and homophobia.

In a 1998 paper on sexism and homophobia toward Asians in the military in the *Minnesota Journal of Law and Inequality*, Julie Yukie

Ralston emphasizes how race and gender are privileged over sexual orientation when fighting for anti-oppression. Ralston concludes, "As long as homophobia continues to be legally sanctioned and socially acceptable, we as a society will not overcome racism or sexism" (668).

REFLECTION QUESTIONS

What stories were new to you? How do you imagine using these narratives in your school or class?

How does intersectionality play in these scenarios? Why is naming the intersectionality important?

Colonization, Colonial Mentality, and Asian American Settler Colonialism

"To understand the root causes of the pathologies we see today, which impact all of us but affect Brown, Black and Poor people more intensely, we have to examine the foundations of this society which began with COLONIZATION....Colonization was the way the extractive economic system of Capitalism came to this land, supported by systems of supremacy and domination which are a necessary part to keep wealth and power accumulated in the hands of the colonizers and ultimately their financiers."

—Dr. Rupa Marya

Every time I lead an anti-bias and anti-racist workshop for schools or companies, I start off with this quote and graph by Dr. Rupa Marya. For this book, I'm leveraging the concept to make others make sense of them and how they intersect the Asian American experience. If colonization is the root cause of supremacism and capitalism, the thought process is to ensure that when embodying an anti-oppressive lens, we are truly embodying an anti-colonial lens (Figure 7.3).

There are many ways to define colonization. In my interpretation, I define colonization as a process where an enterprise takes control of land, power, and resources of another land and its people without consent. When talking about Asian America, we have to acknowledge the colonization of and within Asia, Asians, and Asian America. The "within" is to name the types of colonial

FIGURE 7.3   Colonization map

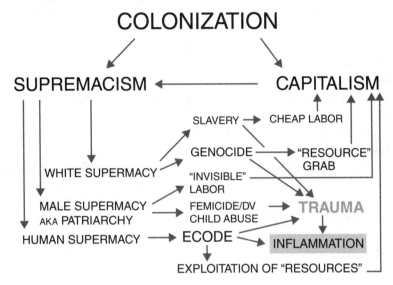

Source: Dr. Rupa Marya

activity with large powers in East Asia attempting to take over land, power, and resources in other parts of Asia (i.e., Japanese colonial rule toward Korea and the Philippines).

There are so many instances one can reference with regard to European colonization toward Asia, but I will focus on a few specific relationships that are tied to my socio-political consciousness and racialization. As a Filipino American, to understand colonization, we must understand the Philippines' relationship to Spain, the United States, and Japan.

The Spanish colonized the Philippines for over 300 years through King Philip II between 1521–1898. This is why our country holds the name "Philippines," it is a literal reminder that Filipinos are from a colonized land and people, which is why some of us identify with the blood of the conquered and blood of the conqueror. Because of the Spanish influence, our names changed, our food changed, our diets changed, our religion changed, and much more.

Next came the United States during their occupation from 1898–1946. The United States claimed to have "saved" the Philippines from colonial rule, but like colonial football, intercepted our land under the sentiment that we were unfit to rule our own lands. They built military bases as a way of instilling Western rule in Southeast Asia. Between 1941–1946, the Japanese started to occupy part of the Philippines to assert its power on the international stage, which led to the Battle of Manila and the "liberation" of the Philippines.

Another legacy of the United States colonialism is the story of male expats and Amerasians. As a result of military men, there are hundreds of thousands of Amerasians, the multi-racial children whose fathers have abandoned them, because they are a direct product of the sex trade in the Philippines during times of war. This group of children and adults are ostracized and are arguably an invisible Filipino group within the Philippines (Choy, 2015).

The point here is that my country is so used to being colonized, occupied, and ruled that there is a level of internalized colonialism that comes with that experience. Scholars call this "colonial mentality."

Colonial Mentality

Colonial mentality is a harmful residue of being colonized. Colonial mentality described by Dr. E.J. David Ramos is an internalized attitude of inferiority as a result of colonization. It makes the colonized feel inferior while propping up the colonizer as the ideal source of value.

From a Filipino American narrative, I recognized this concept during my first trip to the Philippines in 2015. I was awarded grant funding from the Eli Lilly Foundation to study Filipino K–12 urban education. This trip was a rite of passage for me, especially since we idolize the United States as a place to migrate to in order to obtain the "American Dream."

This was also a chance to visit distant relatives in Manila and Pampanga, which are the two regions my family are from. One thing I noticed from my cousin's households was a slew of skin whitening products. On top of skin whitening products, there were many instances where my cousins would casually talk about going to the doctor to get your skin bleached. This blew my mind. It sends the message that our Brown skin is not beautiful or valuable, which again is rooted in anti-Blackness. Colorism is but one aspect of colonial mentality that stems from colonization.

Another aspect from colonial mentality can lead to reproducing colonialism through taking land, power, and control over another already colonized country, which brings me to Asian American settler colonialism.

Asian Settler Colonialism

If settler colonialism is the act of settling into a new place and taking land, power, and resources without consent, this too is happening from Asian Americans through different cultural and political means. Author Tani Loo in the article, "Asian-Settlers Colonialism: Being Chinese in Hawaii," writes what this means from her standpoint. In this article Loo reflects on her Chinese grandparents' history with Hawaii, her positionality as non–Native Hawaiian Asian, and the displacement that occurs when other Asian settlers take root in Hawaii.

One line sticks out, "Epeli Hau'ofa states that we should speak of Oceania instead of the Pacific Islands. They're a sea of islands rather than islands in the sea, and Oceania belongs to no one but itself." This reframing is decolonial. It forces us to reflect on how so much of our language is socially constructed from a white dominant lens. It forces us to grapple with the idea that any visit from an outsider to Hawaii, no matter what background, can be seen as colonial activity. I'm thinking about what Viet Thanh Nguyen stated in his interview in the *Asian American Policy Review*, "Every time you go to Hawaii, for example, you as a tourist, are participating in ongoing colonization and conquest. If you're an Asian American in Hawaii, you are participating in colonization and conquest. How do AAPIs or Asian Americans address that contradiction? That is an emergent and really crucial aspect of our coalition that needs to be at the foreground rather than the background as a part of diversity and inclusion, and the self-congratulatory rhetoric."

Broadly, people do not make that critical connection that participating in the Hawaiian tourism industry perpetuates a colonial and conquest narrative. It perpetuates the false narrative that "Hawaii needs tourism to survive." Asian Americans are not absolved of this, especially if we think about who holds economic, political, and decision-making power pertaining to land allocation in Hawaii.

> **REFLECTION QUESTIONS**
>
> What are your earliest messages of colonialism? How was this formed?
>
> How do you see colonialism show up in your school? Your classroom? Why?

Decolonial Teaching Practices

Rather than linear transactional activities, I offer four methods to help you, your students, and your school's staff become more decolonial toward teaching Asian American narratives and historically marginalized histories as a whole. The first three methods stem from Dr. Miguel Zavala's research entitled, "Decolonial Methodologies in Education" and are shown in Figure 7.4. The last method around permission and consent stems from *Detours: A Decolonial Guide to Hawaii* (Aikau & Gonzalez, 2019).

- ◆ **Counter/Storytelling**: Naming and Remembering. Naming refers to creating the language that allows one to critique the coloniality that exists and operates in our everyday life. Remembering is a form of collective storytelling between past and present in order to root oneself in indigeneity. Both of these are essential in helping re-visibilize the Asian American experience in schools.

  - ◆ What does it look like in practice?

    - ◆ As an educator, I had a living anchor chart that had anti-colonial, anti-bias, and anti-racist terminology. This is a great place to start when thinking about using this as a tool to offer the language of decolonial practice in your room. Regarding counter-stories, I would do this while curriculum planning by ensuring that stories of resistance were always coupled next to stories of oppression that were told through history books. On top of this, I had printouts of Asian American activists in my classroom that served as counter-stories to what was being taught about Asian Americans.

FIGURE 7.4   Decolonial Teaching Practices

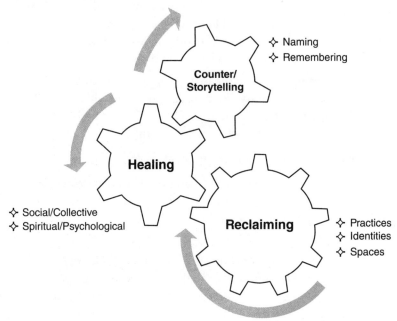

Source: Dr. Miguel Zavala

- ◆ **Healing:** Healing in decolonial education projects entails a particular form of recovering from the historical trauma (physical, social, cultural, spiritual, psychological) experienced by colonized peoples.
  - ◆ What does it look like in practice?
    - ◆ From a healing standpoint, prior to class, I would always start with roses, thorns, and buds in order to get a social-emotional learning check-in.

ROSES	THORNS	BUDS
• (insert something positive that you experienced this week)	• (insert something negative or a tension you've experienced this week)	• (insert something that you look forward to this week)

◆ Naming the thing is healing. When I say that, I mean offering space to ask how Asian American students feel with regard to how class is going. It's important to ask questions like: do you feel included during class? Do you feel like you belong?

◆ **Reclaiming**: This can mean a reclamation of land, nation, and cultural identity. For Native Hawaiians, this relates to the movement #landback, which emphasizes reclaiming the ancestral land from settler colonialism.

   ◆ What does it look like in practice?

      ◆ For me, reclamation can mean exploring what it means to be both Pampangan and Caviteño before being Filipino and American.

      ◆ For Asian American students and staff, we never have the opportunity to reclaim our identities from curriculum being taught or in reclaiming space. May happens to be Asian Pacific Islander American Heritage Month, which is when most schools say *anything* about Asian Americans. Sadly, even within this month, Asian Americans can feel stifled from reclaiming space and time especially if they are one of a few Asian Americans in the building. The stifling comes from the sentiment, "Well there is only like one of me here, so why bother?" That is a scarcity mindset that is taught to Asian Americans and immigrants through the model minority myth frame. Asian Americans are taught to shrink themselves in places of power such as schools and classrooms.

◆ **Permission/Consent:** A decolonial practice means we challenge and strengthen what it means to have consent for land and resources. In Hawaii, mele kāhea is a chant petitioning for entry or welcome and asking permission to enter or pass through a place. One waits for the response, the mele komo, which grants entry and establishes the expectations of pono behavior, gifts, and other forms of reciprocity (Aikau & Gonzalez, 2019, 11–12).

◆ What does it look like in practice?

    ◆ Practicing permission and consent is a daily/ habitual practice that everyone can benefit from. With regard to Asian Americans, they are often pushed into the highest level courses based on the model minority myth. This happened to me when I was in high school when I was pushed into AP classes, when in reality, I should have stayed in traditional courses because the work of AP was too difficult and rigorous for me. No one consulted me if this was the right choice, it was just what was expected of me.

    ◆ Administrators need to consider practicing permission to lead diversity, equity, and inclusion efforts in school. Because many Asian Americans are taught to be deferential, we often take on extra labor without compensation, which again is tied to the model minority myth. Practicing permission and consent from an administrative standpoint means you value our work and time and ask what efforts, beyond teaching, we want and have the capacity to lead.

REFLECTION QUESTIONS

Which of the decolonial practices do you think you accomplish well? Why?

Which of the decolonial practices do you think you need to focus on? Why?

How can you incorporate these decolonial practices sustainably at the school level?

A Movement, Not a Moment

Asian Americans, colonization, colonial mentality, and Asian American settler colonialism can be an entire course taught in schools. There is so much that goes untold from these topics. The following are a few resources I recommend to learn more:

Title/Link	Author(s)	What's in This resource?
Asian-Settlers Colonialism: Being Chinese in Hawaii www.civilbeat.org/2018/12/asian-settlers-colonialism-being-chinese-in-hawaii/#:~:text=Asian%2Dsettler%20colonialism%20is%20when,modern%20cultural%20and%20political%20power.	Tani Loo	This resource offers a reflection from the author about what it means to be a Chinese outsider and settler on Hawaiian soil. It explores how Asian Americans can and do participate in settler colonialism without even knowing it.
A Decolonial Education Takes Shape on Mauna Kea's Ecological University https://truthout.org/articles/a-decolonial-education-takes-shape-at-mauna-keas-ecological-university/	Laurel Mei-Singh & Sarah Marie Wiebe in *Truthout*	This resource offers insight into how Native Hawaiians view Mauna Kea as a place of learning about anti-colonial education.
Native Hawaiian Sovereignty Movement asianamericanedu.org/3.3-Native-Hawaiian-Sovereignty-lesson-plan.html	The Asian American Education Project	This resource offers a few free lesson plans on teaching Native Hawaii's relationship to colonization and the fight for sovereignty.
Decolonial Methodologies in Education link.springer.com/referenceworkentry/10.1007/978-981-287-532-7_498-1	Dr. Miguel Zavala	This resource gives a breakdown on how to use three decolonial methodologies in education.

Chapter 8

Asian American Queer and Trans Perspectives

LEARNING OBJECTIVES:

◆ Practitioners will learn about queer and trans theory (knowledge and mindset).

◆ Practitioners will contextualize queer and trans theory through learning from Asian American perspectives (knowledge).

◆ Practitioners will strengthen their knowledge of intersectionality (knowledge).

The Personal Is Political

"I've lived in our colonizer's lands.
I've spoken my colonizers language,
called myself what they called me: a boy, a "he/she,"
a monster.
But I'm not here to obey your binary.
I'm not here to make you comfortable.
I'm here to free myself. I'm surrendering myself to the
desert wind.
I surrender my body to fire. I burn everything I touch
as I race to freedom. I mean genderqueer.
Genderqueer makes me nobody's son or daughter.
Being genderqueer makes me nobody's lover..."

—*Paul Tran*
Excerpt from the poem "he/she" in Button Poetry

I include this excerpt from Paul's poem "he/she" because it transitions us from the former chapter on colonization and is a beautiful embodiment of resistance toward binary thinking. I want all education practitioners to understand the layers of invisibility as they relate to different intersections of identity and how entrenched binary thinking manifests in education. It's one thing to identify as Asian American and another to identify as Asian American and Queer and/or Trans. As a cisgender heteronormative man, I'm still learning and unlearning how I show up with my fellow Asian American queer and trans siblings, and that does not stop me from teaching about what I have learned up to this point as an ally about Asian American queer and trans perspectives. It should not stop you either.

There is a dangerous neo-liberal logic that says, "If you are not — (insert identity), then don't speak about us." This type of neo-liberal logic keeps change from happening because it puts the responsibility of combating issues pertaining to oppression like transphobia or homophobia on those identifying with queer and trans identities. We cannot afford this type of gatekeeping of knowledge when many schools continue to be systematically unsafe for queer and trans youth.

One example of this can be seen when schools "deadname" students. Deadnaming is when someone refers to a transgender person by the name they were given at birth but no longer use because the name was legally changed. This is the experience that 17-year-old Al Stone-Gebhardt explained in an NPR interview when he was asked about his graduation ceremony. Beyond this, schools are not built to welcome trans youth because they were built without trans and non-binary affirming bathroom structures, let alone a culture that accepts trans and non-binary students and staff.

Early Messages of Gender and Sexual Orientation

I grew up in a large Filipino family, where the term "Baklâ," pronounced as [bɐkˈlaʔ], was often tossed around like colonial football. "Baklâ" translates to gay, gender non-conforming, or third gender in Tagalog. In most cases, the term "Baklâ" was said in a derogatory and dehumanizing way.

What does this do to the psyche? It reinforces the binary around gender and sexual orientation. It conflates both gender and sexual orientation as the same concept. It creates socially constructed rules to abide by, and when one line is crossed, the result is punishment. While I have seen less of this term used in my recent family gatherings, especially with a few of my cousins identifying as queer, trans, or non-binary, the acceptance of these identities and intersections within my family seemed almost haphazard. When thinking about creating a pro–Asian American, pro-queer and pro-trans classroom and school, we cannot take a passive and haphazard approach.

As a parent now, I think about how difficult it is to raise your child in a decolonial and gender-fluid way. The binaries that frame society become all too noticeable as they show up in doctor's visits, clothing stores, daycare, toys, colors, decor, books, and much more. For now, my wife and I have chosen to refer to our child as "our son" to avoid the mental gymnastics. My resistance to the binary is learning more and more about our queer and trans ancestors in the Philippines.

In pre-colonial Philippines times, the Baybaylans (by-by-lans) were and are shamans who often identify as women and/or of the LGBTQIA+ community. They are educators of educators. They were/are held to high esteem next to the Datu (Filipino chieftain) in villages. In Figure 8.1, you'll see a photo of me with Baybaylans in Manila. I had the opportunity to be blessed by Apu Adman Aghama and Lakay Alsent Magbaya during my fellowship at Filipino Young Leadership Program (FYLPRO). Learning about the Baybaylans prepares me to combat toxic masculinity and helps me embrace a more gender-fluid expression. This counter-story helps me unlock language, identities, and ways of being that I did not know I had access to. This ultimately helps me embrace a pro-queer and pro-trans way of being when raising my son.

In the spirit of embracing pro-queer and pro-trans ways of being in schools, I encourage teachers to teach about the third gender

FIGURE 8.1 Tony DelaRosa dressed in his Filipino barong (Filipino traditional clothing). He is being blessed by Apu Adman Aghama and Lakay Alsent Magbaya Aghama in Manila, Philippines.

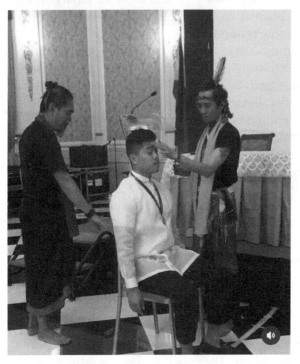

leaders in different Asian communities. In the South Asian community, third gender can be found in Hindu holy texts such as the Ramayana and the Mahabharata. In Indonesia, similar to the Baybaylans, "the bissu bring together woman and man in one person to mediate between humans and gods" (Dresser, 2010). In Malaysia, there were transgender spiritual leaders known as sida-sida, who were entrusted to protect high-ranking women. Unfortunately, due to colonization, there has been a constriction of gender and sexual plurality as power and leadership moved from spiritual leaders to governments and policing bodies (Dresser, 2010).

REFLECTION QUESTIONS

What are your earliest messages of gender and sexual orientation? Were the messages positive, negative, or neutral? How did you come to this realization?

What does the story of the Baybaylans tell us about pre-colonial Philippines?

What does the story of the Baybalyans tell us about leadership?

In this chapter, I introduce some foundational concepts to queer and trans theory and why it came to be. I share some contexts of issues that pertain to the queer and trans community in schools. I charge you to reflect on what this means when we consider the intersections of Asian American identity.

Praxis: Action and Reflection

Throughout my social justice journey in education, I learned by way of being in community with queer and trans leaders, their resistance to the binary of the United States education system, and through the joy of taking up and queering space. The Asian American Avengers, Takeru Nagayoshi and Soukprida Phetmisy, in their recent Smithsonian interview talk about holding a "both/and" mindset, which allows for multiple truths and existences to live and thrive in any given school space. At the University of Wisconsin-Madison, Dr. Kevin Lawrence Henry talks about queering space and practice beyond any form of normative bounds. Mia Nakano's portraits of LGBTQIA+ identifying Asian Americans showcases how art is a form of combating the monolith of Asian Americans and creating a platform for expansiveness.

In the next few pages, I offer two portraits of Asian American activists: Soukprida Phetmisy and Paul Tran. Through their portraits you will learn more about their perspectives and how you can embody a pro–Asian American, pro-queer, and pro-trans way of being for yourself, your class, and your school.

Portraits of Queer and Trans Asian American Artivists

PAUL TRAN (THEY/THEM)

Question: Who are you? What identities and intersectionalities are most salient to you today? What are you working on these days that gives you life?

Born in 1992, I was raised in San Diego, California, by a single-mother who resettled in the United States after escaping Vietnam in 1989. My mother ran a tailoring and dry-cleaning shop where I'd work after school. In that shop, serving as her translator, I saw anything can be made from a pattern and fortified my determination to be the first in our family to graduate high school and attend college. I earned my BA in history from Brown University in 2014 and my MFA in poetry from Washington University in St. Louis in 2019.

While a Wallace Stegner Fellow at Stanford University, I published my first poetry collection, *All the Flowers Kneeling*, with Penguin in 2022. The collection investigates the physical and psychological transformation of a queer and transgender speaker, and thus an autobiographical one, in the aftermath of rape, intergenerational trauma, and war. However, the words "rape" and "trauma" appear nowhere in the book because my poetics, as well as my reason for being a poet and teacher of poetry, is about survival and the audacity, ingenuity, and persistence required to survive. I'm currently an assistant Professor of English and Asian American Studies at the University of Wisconsin-Madison, and I'm working on a second poetry collection about what it's like to be given a second chance. My goal, when I enter the classroom, is to show students that writing and revising a poem is like righting and revising a life. In practicing every element of language and becoming persuasive communicators, we can change not only our stories but also ourselves.

Question: As a writer, performer, and professor what do you want your audience to know when it comes to colonization and the trans and non-binary Asian American experience?

Being alive is miraculous. For me, this has required not only me overcoming my circumstances but also my mother and her mother and hers overcoming all of theirs. Every cell in my body contains our history and taught me that history, like any story, depends on the agenda of the storyteller. My agenda is to show the miracles that my life, and the labors that give my life meaning, empowers me to perform. What else to call the long journey from searching dumpsters for food to scribbling properties of the poetic line on the board in my classroom overlooking Lake Mendota, where I support students on similar journeys, but a miracle? Like turning water into wine, what is a miracle but alchemy, the transformation of a person, situation, or destiny, let's say, into another?

Let it be known that the imperative to be resilient, brilliant every time I speak or think or dare to dream, and to free even the oppressors from themselves has, indeed, made me — and those from backgrounds like mine — resilient, brilliant, and committed to a freedom project that begins with the self.

My miracle, and my story, is the desire to be free, the knowledge that I'm deserving, and the dogged belief that I can do it because generations throughout time have prepared me to be extraordinary for this extraordinary task. Whether or not I actually achieve the freedom I seek, I know, and I want it known, that it's not the achievement but the relentless charge toward freedom and self-actualization that is, ultimately, both the miracle and its proof.

Question: As an educator of Asian American studies, what can practitioners do to embody a pro–Asian American lens when it comes to trans and non-binary experiences?

The term "Asian American" emerges from not only a historical moment of racial and political formation, but also the ongoing experiences of people, places, and things identifying and identified as Asian American.

(Continues)

(Continued)

To practice an Asian American lens in perceiving the world, and oneself in it, is to insist on such experiences as a provenance for examining and producing knowledge about the world, oneself, and perception at large. To be curious about and seek what Asian American people, places, and things reveal about race, class, gender, and sexuality in the United States from contact to present, for example, is to acknowledge the value and realness of Asian American life.

To exclude Asian Americans, as it is to exclude anyone, is to imply that such lives lack value or, worse, that they're not real. What we perceive as real, or unreal, is effectively a matter of imagination. Inclusion or representation is crucial, therefore, because it's about transforming the public and private imagination. It's about perceiving and understanding that those denied of their realness, and their humanity and human rights, are in fact real and rightfully human. It's a resolve to examining and, hopefully, knowing the world more completely, complexly, and thus, more accurately. It's a commitment, actually, to accuracy rather than amnesia and lies that would love to but, in the end, could never pass for knowledge. An Asian American lens at once expands and corrects the imagination, and so the questions for anyone wondering whether such lens would be additive to their work are: How much do you really want to know, why are you afraid to know, and what are you waiting for?

Question: Is there an Asian American ancestor that inspires you? If so, who and why?

In 1982, the writer and filmmaker Theresa Hak Kyung Cha published *Dictee*, a book so complex and otherworldly that it resists being categorized as merely a novel, memoir, or collection of poems. Brought to the United States from Korea as a child refugee, Cha not only explores in *Dictee* the existential wound of exile, but also enacts this wound through language that reveals how a self is made in the absence of a home, homeland, or sense of identity. More importantly, *Dictee* enacts how an estranged self then pursues its own unmaking or remaking.

Although she would not live to see the impact *Dictee* has had on generations of artists and thinkers, Cha has inspired me to be as complex and otherworldly as I want. She reminds me that language must explore and enact, and that my difficulty is my power. I don't need to explain or be understood. I don't need to belong to anywhere or anyone. I don't need to prove anything, and I hardly need to be loved unless it's love on my terms, by my own hard-won definitions. Like *Dictee*, I deserve those who are willing to try — who will stand in the face of mystery and keep looking. Being difficult is difficult, of course, but I'd rather be too much and puzzling and singular and mine than ever again the property of whatever would have me small and easy because its imagination is too diminished to handle me at my fullest, grandest, my most terrifying and terrific.

SOUKPRIDA PHETMISY (SHE/THEY)

Question: Who are you? What identities and intersectionalities are most salient to you today? What are you working on these days that gives you life?

Some days I imagine I am born from fire. A flame within the pit of my mother's belly pushing her toward a different future. When I'm feeling tender, I imagine that fire as a seed of hope. A seed my parents couldn't know would bloom in soil they knew nothing about, yet still, they left all they knew behind for that mere promise of new life. That life is me.

Born in Houston, TX, I was raised by a small, but mighty village of Lao refugees (my mother, father, grandmother, grandfather, and two older sisters) who resettled in the United States after escaping a communist Laos in the late 1980s. Unsurprisingly, my parents' degrees and levels of education didn't transfer to the states (which would later cement the value of education in me in the years to come as being something "no one could take from you" despite systems creating structures that would try).

My mom, an elementary school teacher, and my dad, an electrical engineer, had trouble getting well-paying work. We moved a lot because of it. Sometimes, we moved when my parents got word that other relatives were being resettled in the states. I rarely stayed in the same school for multiple years until we moved to Holland, MI. It took me a long time to formulate a lasting impression and definition of home as a physical place. I've come to, instead, define it as the people around me, which shapes my worldview to this day.

In Holland, MI, I graduated from high school after some formative years of discovering who I was — this soft, curious, weird Lao kid who didn't quite yet have the words to describe desires that felt different than their peers. But through art, mediums like storytelling, performing, and

(Continues)

(Continued)

mixed media, I was able to find language. The arts opened me up so much that I went to college for it despite the dismay of my parents. I earned a BFA in writing from the Savannah College of Art and Design. I zeroed in on courses in sound design because I wanted to audibly tell, preserve, and amplify stories the mainstream didn't seem to center — stories of the global majority.

This practice became my gateway to community organizing and coalition building. It became my tool for self-discovery, activism and artivism, and is what drives my curiosity and critical hope for this work in the day-to-day where (currently) I lead the Asian American and Pacific Islander (AAPI) Alliances in partnerships work with Teach For America. Alongside amplifying AAPI narratives mainstream history has oppressed (especially the stories of impact that AAPI educators have had on students), I have made it part of my life's charge to actively course-correct and disrupt harmful narratives still perpetuated today.

When it comes to the life-giving things, these days I'm working on recapturing stories about the (often unsaid/told) pieces of my ancestry and lineage — an oral history of my family's migration story. I hope to weave it into some kind of quilt or textile that can be passed down with the audio to the next generations as evidence of all the seeds that have bloomed over time in our lineage. On a slightly different tactical side, I am spending the wee hours under the glow of my sewing machine, crafting a capsule wardrobe that'll help me best express my seen identities to the world — like structured wide leg pants and lots of jumpsuits.

Question: As a coalition builder in the Asian American community, what do you want education practitioners across the United States to know when it comes to supporting Asian American queer and trans youth?

Being queer and Asian is a beautiful, expansive thing. There is a collectivist nature to being Asian and there is also one to being queer—there is an ability to traverse multicultural communities in ways that authenticate relationships that are profound and chosen. There is an innate ability to world-build and imagine liberatory spaces that cis-heteronormativity doesn't allow the creativity for. It is special to be at this intersection. I wish I knew and understood that much sooner.

In high school and college, I felt very malleable. I was seeking stories where I could feel seen and heard. I was excited when, in relating to someone else, I discovered new language for a way I felt that helped me better describe who Soukprida is/was in a fuller way. It was in that time I intentionally began exploring my own identities and how I could honor them fully. Some of these markers were easier to claim and embrace — being Lao, being Asian American, being a first generation college kid, growing up low-income, and a child of immigrants/refugees. Some took a little more untangling because of past traumas and deeply internalized fears of othering (especially by loved ones) — accepting my bisexuality, questioning my gender identity, and grappling with my mental health and body dysphoria. Alongside the fear were these glimpses of fullness.

In those days, I'm reminded of the educators and mentors who helped me find ways to explore these curiosities without being intrusive on my boundaries. I think that's important to remember as an adult working with youth — their boundaries are just as valid and important when they're exploring who they are and if they are bringing this to you then you must respect those boundaries completely.

It is, ultimately, remembering they are the experts on themselves. We are guides and relatives along the way. These days it's what feels most salient for me to remember when supporting youth is how I, myself, have not "arrived" and that being a work in progress is not just OK, but valid and very needed to lessen the pressure of societal structures telling us we need to be categorized and labeled at all times.

I share this because I don't think it's ever too late to reclaim a part of yourself or to be gentle with yourself as you evolve your own definitions and understandings of who you are. We are not fixed beings.

Question: Are there organizations, resources, or activities that you lean on when thinking of supporting our nation's educators in embodying a pro–Asian American, pro-queer, and pro-trans lens?

At the heart of ensuring we move with a pro–Asian American, pro-queer, pro-trans lens means seeking out and amplifying counter-narratives to what white supremacy and its structures would have us believe has been lost/erased from our histories about Asian Americans and their unique contributions to this country's past, present, and future. We must ask ourselves (honestly) what resistance we might feel when being asked to adapt these pro-lenses and work toward mitigating that resistance. It is then reconciling with the ways we may not have been pro–Asian American, pro-queer, or pro-trans and holding ourselves accountable to disrupting that. For me, it often comes back to the foundation and health of my home — and as I said

(Continues)

(Continued)

earlier, home is the people around me. Building genuine connection and community with fellow Asian American, queer and trans folks of the diaspora reminds me there is always strength in our collective and our diversity. Taking on a pro–Asian American lens is not a solitary journey, but one of solidarity.

In grounding in that, and with the advantages of the internet and social media, finding and connecting with other queer and Asian education practitioners (and just folks doing cool work, generally) has been made a lot easier. The below are some of the lovely people, organizations, and resources I've leaned on to help me, but by no means is this an exhaustive list:

◆ National Queer Asian Pacific Islander Alliances (NQAPIA)

◆ API Equality NorCal/LA (APIENC)

◆ GAPA (GLBTQ+ Asian Pacific Alliance)

◆ Trikone (for folks of South Asian descent)

◆ Asian Pride Project (http://asianprideproject.org/)

◆ A Day in the Queer Life of Asian America (Smithsonian Asian Pacific American Center)

◆ Dragon Fruit Museum (https://dragonfruitproject.org)

◆ Act To Change

◆ Asian American Education Project (led by Asian Americans Advancing Justice)

◆ A Different Asian American Timeline (https://aatimeline.com)

Question: Is there an Asian American ancestor that inspires you? If so, who and why?

We are not lacking in ancestors despite how much the media may dilute, erase, obscure or hide their stories. They are abundant. I'm constantly drawing on the strength and wisdom of many — Grace Lee Boggs, Patsy Mink, Corky Lee, to name some top of mind. Lately, I've been reflecting on our ancestors in the collective sense and perhaps the mediums left behind or reimagined in new ways. When I think of storytelling and togetherness, I find myself constantly inspired by the students who came together to give us *Gidra.*

In April of 1969, the first issue of *Gidra: The Monthly of the Asian American Experience* was published, issuing the following mission statement: "Truth is not always pretty, not in this world. We try hard to keep from hearing about the feelings, concerns, and problems of fellow human beings when it disturbs us, when it makes us feel uneasy. And too often it is position and power that determine who is heard. This is why *Gidra* was created. *Gidra* is dedicated to truth. The honest expression of feeling or opinion, be it profound or profane, innocuous or insulting, from wretched or well-off — that is *Gidra*. *Gidra* is TRUTH.

Gidra was created to stimulate and inspire members of the Asian American community to vocalize their feelings and thoughts. Many, perhaps Asian Americans included, have come to the conclusion that Asian Americans don't have feelings or thoughts. But we feel that the very existence of a publication like *Gidra* belies the stereotype of the Asian American as a taciturn, unfeeling, and unresponsive individual.

Founded by a group of Asian American students (Dinora Gil, Laura Ho, Tracy Okida, Colin Watanabe, and Mike Murase) from the University of California, Los Angeles, in response to anti-Asian sentiment, it was a self-proclaimed "voice of the Asian American movement." It was revolutionary. It platformed Asian American interests and issues including ethnic studies across universities and the struggles of colonized people in Asia, Africa, and the Caribbean. It is a grounding reminder that this was not too long ago, and yet, here we are still talking about the same things. The original publication ran from 1969–1974 and espoused Third Worldist ideology and collective solidarity. In 2019, with permission from the original creators, it was rebooted. To me, this shows the importance of multigenerational organizing and how past and present and future are so intricately connected. *Gidra* may not have been a person, but it provided a space for a collective community to inhale and exhale together.

REFLECTION QUESTIONS

After reading the two interviews from Paul Tran and Soukprida Phetmisy, what is resonating with you?

What will you take back to your schools from their calls to action?

A Movement, Not a Moment

The theories, practices, reflections, questions, and interviews are a part of an intersectional movement to queer spaces, combat the gender binaries, and create spaces where queer and trans people can thrive. The following are a few resources that influenced this chapter that I urge you to look deeply into:

TITLE/LINK	AUTHOR(S)	WHAT'S IN THIS RESOURCE?
Queer, Trans, and Intersectional Theory www.google.com/books/ edition/Queer_Trans_ and_Intersectional_ Theory_in/4EDCDwAAQ BAJ?hl=en&gbpv=1&printse c=frontcover	Cris Mayo and Mollie V. Blackburn	This resource gives a foundation of queer, trans, and intersectional theory as it relates to K–12 pedagogies.
Is There a Queer Pedagogy or, Stop Reading Straight	Deborah P. Britzman in *Educational Theory* Vol 45.	This resource explores questions of normativity. Queer and trans theory questions the concept of normativity and power.
Making Queer and Trans Asian American Identities Visible www.kqed.org/arts/ 13522854/making-queer- and-trans-asian-american- identities-visible	Sarah Burke in KQED	This resource explores the work of Mia Nakano and the Visibility Project, which is a series of Asian American LGBTQIA+ portraits that enables the subjects to be fully seen.
Queer and Asian Identities www.youtube.com/ watch?v=Ko4V3X4Qc 70&t=1046s	Takeru "TK" Nagayoshi and Soukprida Phetmisy in the Smithsonian Asian Pacific American Center	This resource is an interview that explores what it means to be queer and Asian simultaneously in education.

Chapter 9

Immigration and Undocu–Asian American

LEARNING OBJECTIVES:

◆ Practitioners will define the term undocu–Asian American (knowledge).

◆ Practitioners will unlearn concepts around legality and documentation (mindset).

◆ Practitioners will learn about strategies when teaching students and working with narratives that are undocu–Asian American (skill).

The Personal Is Political

Seed

by Amanda Phingbodhipakkya

We the nation of aliens
Perpetually foreign
Unable to knit together
Open wounds
Of myriad traumas
We dare not bare
Constitutionally refused
Yet here we stand
A legacy of survival
Spread across this land

This poem by Amanda Phingbodhipakkya in her *Very Asian Feelings* exhibition describes how I view the story of my parents, immigration, survival, and education. These concepts were always made clear in how much my parents sacrificed in order for my sister and I to live here and pursue the education we have today. My mom, Ruby DelaRosa, immigrated from Cavite, while my father, Willy DelaRosa, immigrated from Pampanga in the 1980s. I really did not understand who they truly were until I got to visit the Philippines in 2015, and later interviewed them about their immigration story, their pathway to "citizenship," and their journey to the "American Dream." Their story helps me understand what it means to be a child of immigrants and shapes my understanding of the term "undocu–Asian American."

My Experience with Immigration

In 2015 and again in 2018, I had the opportunity to visit the Philippines through both the Ei Lilly Foundation and the Filipino Young Leadership Program (FYLPRO). My journey back to the Philippines feels like a rite of passage as an aspiring Filipino scholar. Many of my Filipino American mentors (and Asian American mentors) in academia share a strong transnational connection between the United States and their motherlands because they often go back to engage with both identities and communities. Many Filipino Americans stay connected to the motherland through the aspect of remittances and embodying the Filipino value of "kapwa," which is a concept that means that all people are interconnected. So you will see many first to second generation Filipino Americans checking in on their relatives in the Philippines. I saw kapwa through my parents.

My parents grew up low income and poor in the Philippines. I don't want to water that down or glorify their conditions. I also don't want to say that they didn't find a sense of joy and pride in the barangay (neighborhoods) that gave birth to them, fed them, and cared for them. But I never understood why they never wanted to go back to the Philippines, and after seeing the lack of resources they survived with, I understand where they are coming from.

In the United States they would find the "American Dream," so why would they want to return to a place that evokes memories of survival? Once my family heard that the United States allowed Filipinos to enlist in the military and immigrate, many of my extended family joined the military and started the process of migration and "legalization." Through this process both of my parents were able to immigrate. The process solidified how they saw the United States military in high regard, and lodged them in a journey of chasing documentation. To be documented was to be "legal." To be "legal" to my parents meant inclusion and belonging. I put terms such as: "the American Dream" and "legalization" in quotations because I want to underscore that these concepts are social constructs just like race.

The brief story of my parents segues us to the concept of "undocu–Asian American." In the "Praxis" section, I include the story of Dr. Rose Ann Gutierrez, who is an assistant professor at the University of Nevada, Reno. She studies race and immigration, and particularly the undocu–Asian American experience. Through reading her story, I include reflection questions that help us build our understanding of what it means to be undocu–Asian American, why that matters, and how to create a class and school that is inclusive of the undocu–Asian American narrative.

Praxis: Action and Reflection

RESEARCHING *WITH* AND *FOR* UNDOCUMENTED ASIAN AND ASIAN AMERICAN STUDENTS

Before I am an assistant professor of Equity and Diversity in Education at the University of Nevada, Reno, I am a daughter—a daughter of immigrants, a daughter of a Caviteño and Cebuana from the Philippines. I am

(Continues)

(Continued)

also an immigrant myself (1.5-generation to be exact). My research sits at the analytical nexus of race, immigration, and education, and I do work with, for, and about undocumented Asian and Asian American[1] students in higher education. Due to my identity as an immigrant and a racialized identity as Asian in the US, I came to my work wanting to understand the stories of undocumented Asian students. Their stories exist, but these stories are often untold and misrepresented in scholarship and public discourse. During my PhD career as a graduate student at the University of California, Los Angeles (UCLA), I conducted a study about undocumented Asian students in higher education without knowing that my reality was closer to the lives of my participants than I had originally thought. In other words, I did not understand the complexity and challenges my own family faced, more specifically, my father's immigration journey regarding his visa application process to the United States. It was only recently, December 21, 2020, that my dad shared with me a small, yet significant, detail in his immigration story that could have changed the entire course of our lives as a family and my own legal status.

Although my mom, Rosita Eborda Gutierrez, and I immigrated to the US from the Philippines in 1997, my immigration story begins with my father's journey. My dad, Potenciano Lingo Gutierrez, came to the US in May 1990 through the family reunification program from his brother's petition. An untold (and unspoken) narrative about my dad's immigration story was the complicated process of needing to create his birth certificate *during* his visa application process for immigration; my dad did not have his birth certificate readily available at the time.

When I was born on December 15, 1989, my dad received paperwork that confirmed his eligibility to immigrate to the United States. This news shocked him because it had been *years* since they filed the paperwork for him to come to the US Understandably so because the United States Citizenship and Immigration Services has had backlogged cases and continues to have backlogs in processing different immigration and renewal applications. What was imperative within this paperwork was a set of instructions that included directions for my dad to submit additional paperwork such as his birth certificate. The problem, however, was that no record existed of my dad's birth certificate in the Municipality of Maragondon in Cavite. You may wonder, "How is that possible?" Well, let us unpack our assumptions about legal documents (e.g., birth certificates)—that they have not always existed, but rather are socially constructed artifacts that we, as a society, give and attach meaning to. As an example, my dad was born in May 1954 in a rural area of the Philippines. During this time, they did not formally record his birth in the system, which would have resulted in a formal document we know as a birth certificate. As my dad shared this story with me, he said, "People were just born."

Now, as we fast-forward to the beginning of 1990, a birth certificate was a necessary document my dad needed to include for his visa application process. Due to this predicament, my dad hired an individual to create his birth certificate to be legally registered in the system in the Philippines. He recalled that this process cost about ₱5,000 Philippine Peso.[2] While my dad shared this part of his story with me, I felt emotions of defeat as he recounted these memories because our family did not have the money at the time. On top of this process, he still needed to pay for the visa application. None of my dad's family members helped or could financially support him. Thankfully, my dad was able to borrow money from a family friend, and he continues to be forever indebted to this family. Throughout the course of our lifetime, not once did this family friend ask for my father to pay them back. Due to this generosity, my dad was able to pay for his birth certificate to be legally created and the visa application. In May 1990, my dad arrived in the United States and settled in Virginia.

My dad did not have a job that entire month of May. He shared how worried he was about my mom and me because he was not able to send us any money for a whole month. When my dad initially immigrated to the United States, he lived in his brother's house, slept on the couch, and then moved to the garage. Finally, a month later, on June 17, 1990, my dad got his first job. He began working multiple part-time jobs from cleaning fish at a restaurant, working as a janitor, and bagging groceries at supermarkets. For four years, my dad saved up money with the goal of returning to the Philippines and marrying my mom. That way, he would be able to begin the paperwork for my mom and me to immigrate to the United States and be with him.

I met my dad for the first time in February 1994, when he came back to the Philippines to marry my mom. I remember a memory of a man, who everyone told me was my father, yet I did not know what a "father" meant in my life because I physically was without one growing up. During this trip, my dad visited the office in Ternate, Cavite, that held records of birth certificates. Due to his experiences of not having his birth certificate in his village's system in the Philippines, he told me that he had a gut feeling about checking my own birth certificate. Upon checking, he was shocked to find out that there was no record of me being born on a birth certificate in the system in Cavite. My dad thought steps ahead regarding the process of petitioning my mom and me to immigrate to the US. Because he had experienced what it took to file his visa application process, my dad made sure to address this issue, so I had the legal documents for immigration when the time came. Three years later, my mom and I reunited with my dad in Virginia Beach, VA, in January 1997 (see Figure 9.1).

(Continues)

(Continued)

FIGURE 9.1 First day of school in the United States, January 1997

No, I am not undocumented, but I am a US-naturalized citizen, who could have been easily undocumented. If my dad had not gone through what he did and taken the steps to have my birth certificate created legally, our immigration story would have looked different. And I am unsure if you would be reading this right now and learning about the stories from the undocumented Asian and Asian American students, whom I got to know and better understand through my research.

As a former PhD student at UCLA, I initially hesitated to touch this subject — the subject of undocumented immigration and more specifically, research about undocumented Asian students. I understood and studied how research had been used and still can operate as a tool in exploiting the stories of vulnerable communities. I did not want to be another researcher to reproduce harm on the lives of an already vulnerable population like undocumented students. As I experienced this dilemma in the first years of my PhD, I connected with an undergraduate student through a colleague. The student expressed how happy they were to meet a Filipina (like them). Additionally, during that initial meeting with the student, they disclosed their undocumented status to me. The student expressed how grateful they were to see someone like me interested in conducting research about undocumented Asian students because they did not know who else to turn to discuss this topic within the realm of research. At that instance, I recalled a quote by Grace Lee Boggs, "If we want to see change in our lives, we have to change things ourselves," which helped me address my dilemma.[3] As mentioned before, research can operate as a tool for exploitation, but I also remembered that I, the researcher, am an instrument within the research process. Because I am an instrument in the research process, I aimed to design my inquiry about undocumented Asian Americans beyond research ethics, but with humanization and healing in mind. Below, I briefly discuss constructing illegality and racialized illegality to help us better understand the experiences of undocumented Asians and undocumented Asian America.

Constructing (Il)legality: The First Undocumented Individuals

"'The problem with living outside the law,' Truman Capote once wrote, 'is that you no longer have its protection.' . . . To pass as an American, I always had to question the law. Not just break it, not just circumvent it, but question it. I interrogate how laws are created, how illegality must be seen through the prism of who is defining what is legal to whom. I had to realize that throughout American history, legality has forever been a construct of power."[4]

The quote above is from Jose Antonio Vargas's book *Dear America: Notes from an Undocumented Citizen*. Prior to delving into this topic, I offer this quote from Vargas to understand that terms like undocumented, illegality, and legality are constructs of power. Sociologist Cecilia Menjívar has written extensively about constructing immigrant "illegality" along with other scholars who have discussed how undocumented status has been a legal and social construction through restrictive immigration laws and policies.[5] In other words, "illegality" or one's undocumented status results from the creation of immigration laws and policies that have been designed to exclude foreigners outside the United States. Take for example, the Chinese Exclusion Act of 1882. The well-known historical fact about the Chinese Exclusion Act was that it barred any persons of Chinese ancestry to enter the United States. However, what is not as deeply and critically discussed are the implications and consequences because of the Act. The Chinese Exclusion Act of 1882 was the first law to bar entry because of race, and more relevant to our current discussion, this Act created who would likely be the first undocumented people—the Chinese.[6] Although no Chinese individuals could enter the US legally as stated through this policy, the Act did not stop the Chinese from physically entering the country to work. In the 1890s, Chinese individuals found other ways to enter the US through the US-Mexico border and Caribbean islands. Additionally, they paid to cross smuggling routes from what we now know as the Vancouver and Puget Sound area in the Pacific Northwest (e.g., $23.00–60.00 USD in the 1890s, which increased up to $300.00 in later decades).[7] Restrictive immigration policies did not stop individuals from coming to the United States. Rather, these policies created an informal economy that profited and exploited immigrant bodies, which we still witness today.

Furthermore, when talking about undocumented Asian and Asian Americans, I use the term "undocumented" versus "unauthorized" or "illegal." I do not use the term "unauthorized," because from my research, I find that the undocumented Asian students I spoke with all came to the United States authorized or *legally*. These students and some of their family members became undocumented by overstaying their visas for various reasons in addition to a complicated visa renewal process.[8] I do not use the term "illegal" because it is a dehumanizing term; people may commit illegal acts due to the ways immigration laws and policies are set up, but people are not inherently "illegal." While I use the term "undocumented," this word still does not capture one's full humanity and dignity. Additionally, individuals who are categorized as "undocumented" in the United States do have documentation, just not the legal documentation that is defined by US law.

REFLECTION QUESTIONS

How does the story that Dr. Rose Ann Gutierrez shares impact on your own definitions of legality?

How does your school combat or reinforce oppressive notions of "legality?"

Racialized Illegality: Omittance from the Contemporary Undocumented Narrative

Although Asians are the fastest growing undocumented racial group in the US, their stories are often untold within the current undocumented narrative.[9] Within the context of higher education, out of the 467,000 undocumented students enrolled at colleges and universities across the country, 25 percent identity as Asian and Pacific Islander,[10] yet scholarship and literature about undocumented Asian and Asian American students remains limited.[11] There are, however, researchers that have begun paving the way for other researchers to build on their scholarship that has focused on undocumented Asian and Asian American students within the past two decades.[12]

Undocumented Asian Americans face a unique form of compounding marginalization that results in their "invisibility." I place "invisibility" in quotes to problematize the term within this discussion for undocumented Asian Americans. The rhetoric of "invisibility" does not capture the form of erasure that speaks to the broader systematic design of how Asian Americans are racialized in US society with an intended form to maintain white supremacy.[13] Moreover, the current undocumented narrative is racialized as a Latin*[14] issue that racially profiles and criminalizes Latin* bodies. While at the same time, Asian Americans are racialized as "model minorities" (as discussed in previous chapters) and often de-minoritized or not considered a minoritized group, which has resulted in exclusion from programs and services designed for minoritized populations.[15] Taken together, due to the intersection of an undocumented Asian's identity (e.g., race and undocumented status), this population is often omitted from the current undocumented narrative and broader discourses of racial equity, which makes it more harmful when we, as a society, do not understand their experiences or even see their existence.

Without attention on undocumented Asians and Asian Americans, US history remains incomplete in its understanding of immigration given the transnational journeys and contributions of Asian Americans that have shaped the United States in the 19th, 20th, and 21st centuries. Reading this chapter is only a glimpse into the topic itself. Due to the ways undocumented Asians and

Asian Americans experience a layered form of marginalization in being omitted from the undocumented narrative and more broadly, racial discourse (as discussed in previous chapters), it is imperative that we continue to unlearn our own preconceived notions and bias about who is included in the undocumented community, educate ourselves about broader topics surrounding immigration that affect Asian American communities like being undocumented, a refugee, and an asylee, and amplify stories about undocumented Asian Americans.

REFLECTION QUESTIONS

When you think about the term undocumented, what race first comes to mind? Why?

Why does Dr. Rose Ann Gutierrez use the term "omission" over "invisibility" to describe Asian Americans?

A Movement, Not a Moment

This is a place for additional resources to continue learning.

If I could go back to the drawing board, I would title this book "Teaching the Omitted Race..." I learned so much from listening and studying Dr. Rose Ann Gutierrez's story, research, and breakdown of the term "Undocu–Asian American." Here you will find more resources to continue your learning on this layered topic:

Title/Link	Author(s)	What's in This Resource?
Dear America: Notes of an Undocumented Citizen	Jose Antonio Vargas	This resource shares about the undocu–Asian American experience through storytelling.
Impossible Subjects: Illegal Aliens and the Modern Making of America	Mae M. Ngai	This resource gives more historical context on undocu–Asian America.

Title/Link	Author(s)	What's in This Resource?
Immigrants Rising, immigrantsrising.org	n/a	This resource goes into a variety of services and programs on how to navigate while being "undocumented." This includes strategies to navigate finances, college, mental health, well-being, and more.
AAPI Data aapidata.com/ undocumented/		This resource offers data on where undocumented Asian American populations reside.

Notes

1. I use "Asian(s) and Asian American(s)" as two separate terms to make a distinction that not all Asian individuals identify with the political panethnic identity of "Asian American." In my study, some participants identified as Asian while others identified with the political panethnic identity as Asian American. I do not use aggregated terms and other political panethnic identities such as Asian American and Pacific Islander (AAPI), Asian Pacific Islander (API), Asian and Pacific Islander American (APIA), and Asian Pacific American (APA) to avoid erasing experiences of Pacific Islanders within a panethnic identity and reproducing a narrative of these groups as a homogeneous group in the conversation of race and racialization (Gogue et al., 2022). I do use aggregated terms and panethnic identities if previous data sources I cite have used the terms.
2. In 1990, the conversion rate from the Philippine Peso (PHP) to the US Dollars (USD) on average was ₱22.71 to $1.00 (Department of the Treasury, 1990).
3. Boggs, G. L. (2011). *The next American revolution: Sustainable activism for the twenty-first century.*
4. Vargas, J. A. (2018). *Dear America: Notes of an undocumented citizen.* HarperCollins.

5. Menjívar, C., & Kanstroom, D. (Eds.). (2013). *Constructing immigrant "illegality": Critiques, experiences, and response.* Cambridge University Press.

6. Ngai, M. M. (2004). *Impossible subjects: Illegal aliens and the modern making of America.* Princeton University Press.

7. Lee, E. (2015). *The making of Asian America: A history.* Simon & Schuster Paperbacks.

8. Gutierrez, R. A. R. E. (2022). *Racialized realities at the intersection of race and undocumented status: A critical narrative inquiry into the lives of undocumented Asian students in higher education* [Doctoral dissertation, University of California, Los Angeles]. ProQuest Dissertations Publishing. https://escholarship.org/uc/item/0307x0ff

9. Kim, S. M., & Yellow Horse, A. J. (2018). Undocumented Asians. *Contexts, 17*(4), 70–71.

10. I use the term "Asian and Pacific Islander" to reflect the same language used in the original reporting of the data from the March 2021 report about undocumented students in higher education by The Presidents' Alliance on Higher Education and Immigration. The data in the report aggregates undocumented Asians and Pacific Islanders.

11. Feldblum, M., Hubbard, S., Lim, A., Penichet-Paul, C., & Siegel, H. (2021). *Undocumented students in higher education: How many students are in U.S. colleges and universities, and who are they?* The Presidents' Alliance on Higher Education and Immigration.

12. Buenavista, T. L. (2018). Model (undocumented) minorities and "illegal" immigrants: Centering Asian Americans and US carcerality in undocumented student discourse. *Race, Ethnicity and Education, 21*(1), 78–91. Buenavista, T. L., & Chen, A. C. (2013). Intersections and crossroads: A counter-story of an undocumented Pinary college student. In S. D. Museus, D. Maramba, & R. Teranishi (Eds.), *The misrepresented minority: New insights on Asian American and Pacific Islanders, and their implications for higher education* (pp. 198–212). Stylus Publishing. Cho, E. Y. (2019). *Invisible illegality: The double bind of being Asian and undocumented* [Doctoral dissertation, University of California, Berkeley].

ProQuest Dissertations Publishing. https://escholarship
.org/uc/item/0nk070sx. Enriquez, L. E. (2019). Border-hopping
Mexicans, law-abiding Asians, and racialized illegality:
Analyzing undocumented college students' experiences through
a relational lens. In N. Molina, D. M. Hosang, & R. A. Gutiérrez
(Eds.), *Relational formations of race: Theory, method, and practice*
(pp. 257–277). University of California College Press. Gutierrez,
R. A. R. E. (2022). *Racialized realities at the intersection of race and
undocumented status: A critical narrative inquiry into the lives of
undocumented Asian students in higher education* [Doctoral dissertation, University of California, Los Angeles]. ProQuest
Dissertations Publishing. https://escholarship.org/uc/item/
0307x0ff. Salinas Velasco, C. F., Mazumder, T., & Enriquez, L. E.
(2015). "It's not just a Latino issue": Policy recommendations to
better support a racially diverse population of undocumented
students. *InterActions: UCLA Journal of Education and Information
Studies, 11*(1), 1–11.

13. Okihiro, G. (1994). *Margins and mainstreams: Asians in American
history and culture*. University of Washington Press. Park, L. S. H.
(2008). Continuing significance of the model minority myth: The
second generation. *Social Justice, 35*(2), 134–144. Wu, F. H. (2002).
Yellow: Race in America beyond Black and White. Basic Books.

14. I use the term Latin* to consider individuals who identify as
Latina, Latiné, Latino, Latina/o, Latin@, Latinx, Latin, or Latin
American (Salinas, 2020). Salinas introduces the * (asterisk) in
"Latin*" as a deliberate intervention or to create pause for read-
ers to consider the multiple ways in which people from Latin
American origin and diaspora in the United States identify at the
intersection of race, ethnicity, culture, gender, sexuality, geogra-
phy, language, and phenotype.

15. Lee, S. S. (2006). Over-Represented and De-Minoritized: The
Racialization of Asian Americans in Higher Education.
*Interactions: UCLA Journal of Education and Information Studies,
2*(2), 1–16.

Chapter 10

Asian Americans, Disability Narratives, and Crip Ecology

- ◆ Practitioners will learn about basic disability education theory and crip ecology (knowledge).

- ◆ Practitioners will learn from disabled Asian American narratives (knowledge and mindsets).

- ◆ Practitioners will leave with considerations and ways of combating ableism as it pertains to Asian Americans in schools (skills).

The Personal Is Political

"If we made more of our poetry and art spaces accessible, if we invested in caring for the poet more than their output or productivity, how would it change people's experiences of poetry and of nature? How would people's fear of becoming disabled shift if instead disabled was understood as a way of being and becoming, an opportunity for illumination?"

—*Kay Ulanday Barrett*

"The day will come when crip world will be the only world that survived. Crips will do anything to survive and that's what they want to deny when they kill us...our will to live is greater than your ability to get rid of us.
    —*Maria R. Palacios, Sins Invalid, "We Love Like Barnacles"*

*Disclaimer: I use the term "crip ecology" throughout this chapter as an able-bodied person because it is a critical concept from Kay Ulanday Barrett's essay that grounds this chapter.

When I think about the opening poem of my book *How will you hold us?* I think about two people: 1) Rain Fuertes (my cousin), and 2) Kay Ulanday Barrett (poet and educator). My cousin Rain was diagnosed with Autism and ADHD. My auntie Arlene Fuertes is Rain's mother and full-time caretaker. She is a fierce advocate for youth on the autism spectrum and educates the community on the journey of being Rain's parent and how to take on a pro-autism and pro-disability lens through her Instagram account @braveheart_autism03. As I write this, I'm looking at one of her posts that cites *Autism Parenting Magazine* to celebrate April's Autism Awareness month: "Autism is about having a pure heart and being very sensitive. . . It is about finding a way to survive in an overwhelming, confusing world. . . It is about developing differently, at a different pace and different leaps." Auntie Arlene pulled Rain out of formal education, because United States public education is that "overwhelming and confusing world." As I write this chapter, I think about all the parents/guardians who have to make the impossible decision to pull their kids from formal public education, because these spaces are not designed to adequately serve students with individualized education plans (IEPs). To a similar sentiment, poet and educator Kay Ulanday Barrett shares how their "crip ecology is directly connected to [their] pace and place."

Kay Ulanday Barrett's 2022 essay published by the Poetry Foundation, "To Hold the Grief & the Growth[1]: On Crip Ecologies". As a queer trans disabled Filipinx American poet, Kay describes the grief of having to navigate the "literary world" (and the world at large) that values capitalism and exceptionalism, which are two concepts that directly perpetuate harm and barriers to access. Capitalism and exceptionalism are connected to the model minority myth, because the terms for success under each system and concept are defined by white dominant values. If we think about Asian Americans and disability narratives, the perpetual foreigner stereotype can feel extra heavy because people with disabilities are treated as "foreign" to what able-bodied people deem as "normal" or "domestic." And when we think about these enmeshing identities, we return back to the concept of "the invisible within the invisible." But poets and educators like Kay refuse to live in the deficit lens.

Kay's question "How would people's fear of becoming disabled shift if instead disabled was understood as a way of being and becoming, an opportunity for illumination?" is a vital reframing and invitation to challenging notions of exceptionalism, capitalism, fear economics, the model minority myth, the perpetual foreigner stereotype, and embracing disability as something that we are all connected to—after all the majority of us may enter the world as able-bodied but may experience disability in different points of life, especially as we get older.

The second quote from Maria R. Palacios is cited in Kay's essay, centers on the willpower of the crip community. The term "crip," growing up, was always associated with something derogatory as in the imagery of "being crippled." Thanks to Dr. Kevin Lawrence Henry's CRT in Education class at UW-Madison, I've learned that the term "crip" is being reclaimed by some disabled communities and people. In their essay, Kay writes:

> "Crip ecologies, crip time, crip ingenuity, crip spirit radically aim to question root systems that keep our imaginations limited and starved. How can we channel joy within our own skins before there is the stethoscope, the specialist's jackhammered interrogation, before all the stigma we battle? I am not asking to look beyond it, because these constraints in our beings are here and ever-present. I am asking, as poets, as curious people who want liberation, how do we revel in the grief and also the growth we experience?"

After reading this, I couldn't help but think about Dr. Kevin Quashie's book *In Black Aliveness, or A Poetics of Being*. In the book, Quashie challenges readers to embrace a Black Aliveness framework that embodies the concept of wholeness, being, and becoming. Quashie acknowledges that Blackness and death are always enmeshed, so we need a framework that is expansive, radical, futuristic, and alive. Similarly, for Kay, crip ecology allows for expansiveness, radicality, futurism, and aliveness. Before I end this section of this chapter, I must add that disability activist, Petra Kuppers, explains in a 2022 Poetry Foundation essay entitled "Crip Ecologies: Changing Orientation" that the term has become "too ubiquitous" as it is often used in academia by non-disabled people who benefit from the concept through getting paid to speak about it or by other means. Kuppers challenges the able-bodied community by stating ". . .when you use the term "crip," stay aware of who is in the room, and who is not, and how you can enlarge the circle."

> **REFLECTION QUESTIONS**
>
> What is resonating with you as you read part of Rain's and Kay's stories?
>
> What does crip ecology tell us about the United States education system?
>
> How does crip ecology connect to Asian American narratives?

Praxis: Action and Reflection

After reading about Rain, Kay, and crip ecology, for this "Praxis" section, I hand the torch off to my friend Miso Kwak, who is a special education scholar and disability justice activist. Miso and I attended Harvard together at different times, yet we ended up at UW-Madison pursuing our PhDs at the same time and now work together to advocate for Asian American liberation through education. In this section she shares her story and tangible ways education actors can take on a pro–Asian American and pro-disability lens in their work at schools.

Paradox is a word that comes to mind when I reflect on my upbringing as a 1.5-generation Korean American disabled person. I remember recognizing many opportunities that being in America afforded me yet not knowing how to access them due to linguistic, cultural, and systemic barriers. I remember trying to make sense of the ways in which adults expected me to excel in school because I am Asian yet holding me back because of low expectations toward disabled students. I remember feeling the pressure to find my niche, a place where I would not have to try so hard to prove something to other people...just to exist as my full self.

It is with this reflection that I approach writing this "Praxis" section for this chapter. I also would like to note that I use identity-first (e.g., disabled students) and person-first (e.g., students with disabilities) interchangeably. Doing so recognizes that each person has a different and complicated relationship with disability.

This "Praxis" section includes the following:

♦ Ensuring linguistic competence

♦ Ensuring cultural competence

♦ Increasing representation of Asian American with disabilities

♦ Paying attention to the invisible within the invisible

Ensure Linguistic Competence

If the student and/or their parents' primary language is not English, find out in advance whether they will need an interpreter for the IEP meeting. The Individuals with Disabilities Education Act (IDEA) requires that the parent understands the IEP meeting. If needed, take the necessary steps to arrange an interpreter. Also, make sure that the interpreter is familiar with the language used in the IEP meeting and understands anti-ableist practices.

Ensure Cultural Competence

It is equally important to be culturally competent when working with students with disabilities and their parents who are Asian American. Disability is often associated with stigma for many, regardless of their racial and ethnic backgrounds. However, it is important to understand the nuances of ableism in the Asian American community. For example, Sandy Ho, an Asian American disabled woman wrote in her essay titled "Canfei to Canji: The Freedom of Being Loud" how the Chinese words used to talk about disability "canfei" meaning "useless" and "canji" meaning sickness shaped her relatives' perception of her upon being born disabled. Associating disability with "useless" or "sickness" because of the language may be an obstacle to adopting the more legal, rights-based framework that schools often use when providing support and services for students with disabilities in the US. In addition, students may have more difficulty as they grapple with their own disability identity and Asian American identity as they may seem to be conflicting.

Another nuanced understanding of disability particular to the Asian American community can be found in Anne Fadiman's book, *The Spirit Catches You and You Fall Down: A Hmong Child, Her*

American Doctors, and the Collision of Two Cultures. Fadiman wrote
about Foua Yang and Nao Kao Lee, Hmong refugees whose young-
est daughter had epilepsy. Unlike American doctors who viewed
epilepsy as a disabling medical condition, Foua and Nao Kao
viewed epilepsy as both an illness and a divine blessing, considering their daughter as an anointed one. This reflects traditional
Hmong beliefs that a person with epilepsy or similar condition has
the potential to become a shaman.

These are just a few examples of different beliefs about disability
that students and their parents may hold, influenced by language
and culture. What is important as educators is to listen and learn
from students and their parents, and offer support to maximize the
opportunities for the student and their parents.

Increase Representation of Asian Americans with Disabilities

One of the best ways to offer support for Asian American students
with disabilities and their parents is by increasing representation
of disabled Asian Americans in the classroom. Highlight the
work of disabled Asian Americans who are working in various
sectors. Encourage students and parents to learn about the Asian
American disabled activists. If possible, connect your students with
older students and encourage them to build a relationship.
Similarly, encourage parents to connect with other parents of
disabled students.

Here are some resources:

◆ *Mia Lee is Wheeling Through Middle School* by Melissa Shang
  and Eva Shang

◆ *Disability Visibility Adapted for Young Adults*, edited by Alice
  Wong (A full version also exists; a few of the authors featured are Asian Americans)

◆ Center for Parent Information and Resource [Not AAPI
  specific, though I think some of the centers have some Asian
  language supports (e.g., California has a center with staff
  who can support Chinese-speaking parents)]

Pay Attention to the Invisible Within the Invisible

Some disabilities are apparent and the identification is largely dependent on verifiable biological data, like physical or sensory disabilities. Some disabilities, however, like specific learning disability or emotional behavioral disability, on the other hand, depend on clinical judgment for identification. Black, Latine, and Native American students are overrepresented in special education, particularly in learning disability and emotional behavioral disability. This phenomenon reflects racist biases in IQ testing and disciplinary practices in school (Harry & Klingner, 2022).

When it comes to Asian American students, however, Wang et al. (2021) found that educators are less likely to refer Asian American students for learning disability evaluation when they struggle in reading or math, compared to their white counterparts. Cooc (2019) also found that most AAPI groups are underrepresented in special education, and access special education services later than their white peers. Be mindful of such trends; pay attention to your students and examine biases you might have because of the belief that Asian American students tend to be shy or quiet and are supposed to excel in school. Do you notice any students, particularly Asian American students, struggling academically and/or behaviorally? Could those students benefit from receiving extra support that could be afforded through special education?

A Movement, Not a Moment

In this chapter, you read about my auntie's relationship to her son Rain and how she challenges people to reframe how they approach people with autism and ADHD. You read about Kay Ulanday Barrett's work with crip ecologies learning how they hold both grief and growth simultaneously in "the apocalypse" that is an ableist world. Finally, you ended the chapter meeting Miso Kwak, a special education scholar and disability justice activist, who shared her story and tangible ways to approach schools with a pro–Asian American and pro-disability lens.

Here is a list of resources that Miso and I recommend to strengthen your knowledge to better serve students with disabilities at your school:

TITLE/LINKS	AUTHOR(S)	WHAT'S IN THIS RESOURCE?
Not a Unicorn: Finding Communities Within a Community https://smithsonianapa .org/now/finding-communities-within-a-community-americans-with-disabilities-act/	Alice Wong	In this essay, disability justice activist and media maker Alice Wong writes about the need to increase AAPI disability representation, two narratives that reflect the intersection of being AAPI and disabled, and draws the parallel between the disability community and AAPI community.
A Letter to My Younger Self https://www.nmdunited .org/single-post/ss-aubrie-lee	Aubrie Lee	This is a moving narrative written by a Chinese-American disabled activist. It would be a great piece to introduce to disabled students [suited for secondary level] and parents alike.
Remaking a World That Wasn't Built for Us: On South Asian American Disability Activism https://www.saada.org/ tides/article/remaking-a-world	Harshada Rajani	This essay captures the experiences of living in the intersection of being South American and being disabled.
The Asian Americans with Disabilities Initiative (AADI) https://www.aadinitiative .org/	Jennifer Lee [founder]	This is a youth-led nonprofit organization that aims to uplift disabled Asian American voices. Check out the resources guide and follow them on Instagram.
Critical Disability Studies Collective: Terminology https://cdsc.umn.edu/ cds/terms	The Critical Disability Studies Collective at the University of Minnesota	This resource provides critical disability studies terminology.

Part 3

Teach Us Visible by Celebrating Us

Chapter 11

Teaching Us Visible Through Art, Poetry, and Hip-Hop

LEARNING OBJECTIVES:

- ◆ Practitioners will learn of Asian American artists (knowledge).

- ◆ Practitioners will learn how to teach Asian American studies through art (skill).

The Personal Is Political

"Before I ever wrote a poem, I stood in a prayer circle with my friends and traded rhymes. A prayer circle. Yes. Cipher-as-prayer, as witness that your words can call down thunder and resurrection if you believe in them hard enough."

—Michael Mlekoday

"Without question, I am a child of hip-hop."

—t'ai freedom ford

These two quotes are pulled from artist statements from *The BreakBeat Poets: New American Poetry in the Age of Hip-Hop.* When I think about combating white supremacy's insidious grip on the Asian American image in America, I think about the power of art, poetry, and of course hip-hop. Like Michael Mlekoday, hip-hop offered a communal and spiritual space for me, and similar to t'ai freedom ford: "I am a child of hip-hop."

Black resistance and joy birthed hip-hop in the Bronx circa 1973 by Clive Campbell, or famously known as DJ Kool Herc (aka the father of hip-hop). Hip-Hop exploded because of Black culture; it transcended into a global artform and language. Growing up in Oceanside, California, I witnessed this power through so many

Asian Americans adopting hip-hop and performing it in community with the Black community. One prominent example was my
older cousins: Timothy Caballero and Anthony Williams. I witnessed them breakdancing, cyphering, transforming the mundane,
and erased into art. It was alchemy. They would collaborate too,
two Filipino Americans taking up as much sound and space as their
hearts desired. Similar to other hip-hop stories, in our large
extended Filipino family, Timothy and Anthony were not often
talked about from the white dominant lens that characterizes
"intelligence" — but they were and are in fact brilliant. At such a
young age they were both artists, leaders, community builders, and
entrepreneurs. Of course, a young blood like myself at the time
would follow suit.

Plot twist — I was never good at hip-hop, until I found spoken
word through the work of Saul Williams and Beau Sia who performed in Def Poetry, a television series hosted by Mos Def, produced by Russel Simmons and aired on HBO between 2002 and
2007 (see Figure 11.1). Saul Williams rooted me in Black liberation,
while Beau Sia contextualized what this could mean for Asian
Americans.

FIGURE 11.1 Tony DelaRosa next to Saul Williams at Cedarville University

In spoken word poetry, I found three things:

◆ My artistic voice

◆ My critical consciousness

◆ A community

The spoken word aesthetic worked better for me as my voice and sense of identity matured at open mics. I did my first spoken word performance at Baba Budan's, a local bar near the University of Cincinnati (UC). A Black artist and community organizer, Rome Ntukogu, put me on the list, heard me spit a few lines of a poem and from there — I became a spoken word poet. Never in a million years would I think of myself as a spoken word poet until that moment. Before then, my conception of Asian Americans was limited through seeing us in kung-fu films and the passive subject of US history; essentially Black culture provided me with a platform and the tools to change that.

After graduating from UC, I joined the PreK–12 teaching force and brought this passion into action by co-founding a city-wide spoken word youth organization called Indy Pulse in Indianapolis. At this time in my life, my inspiration was Dr. Christopher Emdin who currently serves as the Robert A. Naslund Endowed Chair in Curriculum & Teaching at the University of Southern California. Dr. Emdin has influenced my pedagogical lens and the way in which I think about the role of school and community. First, Dr. Emdin challenges the concept of "classroom management." Many programs today train teachers how to "manage behavior and with Dr. Emdin theory of Reality Pedagogy asserts that we must view students as teachers, share power, and co-generate learning together. On a community level, Dr. Emdin founded "Science Genius," an organization that provides spaces and resources for young scientists to realize and cultivate their gifts through hip-hop. Like Science Genius, Indy Pulse worked with Black and Brown youth, cultivating their voice and sense of critical consciousness. One of our Indy Pulse poets, Alyssa Gaines, even became the US National Youth Poet Laureate and attends Harvard University. This is one example of the power of art and education. My Asian American Artist story is one of many. In the next section, you'll read more about the history of Asian Americans, Art History, Racism, and Resistance.

Asian Americans, Art History, and Racism

It's worth noting that Asian Americans have fought to create and maintain our image as beautiful, human, and multifaceted. When our images are used by people who don't understand the Asian American political story, you get distorted and racist imagery that leads to concepts of "Orientalism" and "Yellowface." According to Brown University professor of American studies Robert G. Lee, orientalism has six specific tropes:

◆ the pollutant (the alien presence, which spreads through American society)

◆ the coolie (cheap foreign labor)

◆ the deviant (unassimilable opium den dweller and prostitute

◆ the yellow peril (the threat of coolies stealing jobs from working-class Americans)

◆ the model minority (as opposed to Blacks and Hispanics)

◆ the gook (the generic Asian wartime threat), which "portray the Oriental as an alien body and a threat to the American family"

Yellowface, like Blackface, is when a non–Asian American dresses up like an Asian American and mimics a singular, stereotypical, and harmful archetype of Asians. Yellowface can also be defined as anyone playing the role of an Asian character that is not Asian. Orientalism and yellowface were commonly used in movies such as *Breakfast at Tiffany's (1961)* and *Miss Saigon (1981)*. Today, we see yellowface in Paramount Studio's 2017 live-action adaptation of classic Japanese anime *Ghost in the Shell*, Marvel's 2016 *Dr. Strange,* Dune Entertainment's 2006 *Dragonball: Evolution,* and Paramount Picture's 2018 *Annihilation.*

Orientalism found its way in children's books through Western imperialism. The most common example that people would not think of is Dr. Seuss. The US military hired popular artists like Dr. Suess to create anti-Asian war propaganda invoking the perpetual foreigner threat. When you think of children's literature, Dr. Suess undoubtedly comes to mind because of his famous works that have been translated into movies, toys, apparel, and much more. Dr. Seuss is a worldwide enterprise. But Dr. Seuss had a dark and racist side to his work.

He explicitly degraded Black, Indigenous, Asian, Muslim, Jewish, and others historically and systemically marginalized people through his work (Ishizuka & Stephens, 2019, 1). In a Dartmouth analysis by Hannah Cho, she describes how Dr. Seuss used orientalism to portray Emperor Hirohito next to Hitler. She states, "the Japanese man in this cartoon is portrayed with a pig snout, a mustache similar to Hitler's mustache, buck teeth, glasses, and squinted eyes. Having just come off of World War I, the American people's disgust and hatred of Hitler were used as fuel in this cartoon to transfer the detest of Hitler to the Japanese people, represented by Emperor Hirohito in this caricature. The depiction of Emperor Hirohito as the "typical" Japanese man also causes the Japanese to lose their identity as individuals and to instead be seen as a collective group of enemies."

REFLECTION QUESTIONS

Have you seen images of orientalism or yellowface? Where and what context did you learn these from?

Did you know that authors like Dr. Suess produced anti-Asian war propaganda? What does this bring up for you?

Art, War, and Fetishism

Outside of orientalism and yellowface, art has been used to perpetuate exoticism and fetishism toward Asian American women in the context of war. An example of this fetishism is through Giacomo Puccini's famous opera, *Madama Butterfly.* This opera portrays a white naval officer named John Pinkerton who gets stationed in Japan and meets a 15-year-old Geisha named Butterfly. They eventually marry and have a son. When Pinkerton returns to the United States, he marries a white woman named Kate, and eventually sends Kate to retrieve his son. Out of devastation and heartbreak, Butterfly commits suicide.

Madama Butterfly is reminiscent of military men going to Asia, "falling in love" with an Asian sex worker, having a child, and the privilege of leaving. The musical *Miss Saigon* is another version of this story set in Vietnam. Madama Butterfly continues in the Philippines, at Clark Air Force Base in Angeles City through Filipina sex workers. "The American Dream" of being saved by marrying a white foreigner is a tragic story for Filipina who want to escape sex-trafficking and forget a past of poverty and exploitation. This opera is still in production today at places like the San Francisco and Metropolitan Opera.

The past fetishization of Asian American women connects to the present day anti-Asian hate toward Asian American women when we think about the Atlanta Spa Shootings in 2021. On March 16, 2021, out of eight people murdered in the Atlanta Spa shootings, six Asian American women were killed in the name of "sex addiction." Brown University Professor Elena Shih and UCLA Professor Lee Ann Wang discuss how this murder spree reinforces the fetishization and commodification of Asian American women. The organization Stop AAPI Hate reported that 68 percent of the anti-Asian violence reported to them came from women.

REFLECTION QUESTIONS

Knowing that Asian American women are more likely to report anti-Asian violence, what is coming up for you when it comes to embodying a pro–Asian American lens in schools?

Art, Reclamation, and Resistance

Asian Americans, similar to myself, have used art, poetry, and hip-hop to reclaim their identities from white supremacy. You see this through art that protests white supremacy, art that moves away from the white gaze, and art that centers the Asian American community. Some examples of this type of art are found in UCLA's Asian American newspaper—*Gidra* (1969–1974), Tam Tran's visual collection "Accents" (2009), the Smithsonian Asian Pacific Center's "Beyond Bollywood" (2014–2015), and Amanda Phingbodhipak-kiya's "Very Asian Thoughts" (2022).

In this next section, I include an interview of artivists Ruby Ibarra and Amanda Phingbodhipakkiya, along with activities and reflection questions you can use with your school. They represent a contemporary group of Asian American Avengers that use art as a form of self-exploration and subversion.

Poetry and Hip-Hop

As noted in my story about becoming a spoken word poet, I had the pleasure of interviewing Ruby Ibarra who is a Filipina Ameri-can rapper, poet, director, and scientist. I first encountered her work when listening to her on a cypher on YouTube produced by a company called Team Backpack in 2011. From there, my connection to Ruby's work grew, until we would find ourselves in similar arts, education, and activist spaces.

INTERVIEW WITH RUBY IBARRA

Question: Who are you? What identities and intersectionalities are most salient to you today? What are you working on these days that gives you life?

I'm a songwriter. I'm a poet. I'm a daughter. I'm a sister. I'm an artist. I think the identities that are most salient to me are being Filipino and being a woman. These identities are reflected in a lot of the topics and themes that I talk about in my music and in my poetry, and I feel that

---

(Continues)

(Continued)

they're most important because of growing up as a Filipino American in the United States as an immigrant. These were the identities that I often used to navigate – the spaces that I was in, whether that was coming to terms with who I was and how I should interact with others and how I saw myself ultimately, in this puzzle called America.

My sophomore album gives me life and other pieces of literary work that I'm currently working on. They give me life because they are a true reflection and expression of who I am and where I come from. When I make my music, I always make it a point to never forget who the person is behind the microphone. I think ultimately I became a big hip-hop fan because of artists such as Tupac Shakur and Lauryn Hill, where I got a glimpse of who they were. I got a glimpse of what their life was like. I think if it wasn't for artists like that, I wouldn't know who I am.

Question: What was your experience like in PreK–12 education? Did you see Asian Americans reflected in the curriculum or your school?

I did not see Asian Americans reflected in the curriculum. I don't even think that I ever saw Asian Americans mentioned in any of my history classes until I was in high school. If anything there was a brief mention of Chinese Americans and the railroad system in the United States found in a short paragraph in my Advanced Placement US History class. For the longest time, I didn't feel connected to not only my Asian American identity, but more specifically my Filipino American identity because I didn't realize there was this void in our representation in the educational curriculum. I didn't know who I was, I didn't know how to trace my identity back. It wasn't until I was 18 years old, as a freshman at UC Davis when I took an Asian American studies course where I finally learned about Asian American history. It shouldn't take someone 18 years to learn who they are and what their community's history is like.

And in addition to that, I remember every year in elementary school, I would hate the first day of school because this was the introduction for teachers to learn not only who you are, but what your name is, and I would always dread whenever it would come down to the roll call at the start of the class because I knew ahead of time that the teacher would completely butcher my name. I think that early on, you know, taught me that my identity and my name were classified under the "other," that I was foreign and I never really felt like my other classmates who had American names.

Question: How do you use hip-hop as reclamation or resistance?

When I first wrote my songs, I used Filipino as my special card to stand out. Today, when I write songs, such as "Playbills" or "US," I make sure to include Filipino language in it because the overarching theme of the record was about my story as a Filipino immigrant. I couldn't accurately portray my story if the Filipino language wasn't part of it, because growing up that's what we spoke in my household. Filipino is also something that I use to still maintain ties to my Filipino culture and the Philippines. I know young Filipino Americans who are taught not to speak or learn the language. I saw this firsthand with my younger sister. I grew up speaking and understanding Visaya as well as Tagalog in my household, but my younger sister who's three years younger than me, never learned how to speak the languages on purpose. My parents chose not to teach my younger sister because they thought that it would be difficult for her to assimilate in American culture.

Using the Filipino language in my music is a celebration of Filipino culture. It is also an educational tool for me to show people that just because you don't utilize English in your works, it doesn't make it any less valid. It doesn't make it any less legitimate. That's what I use in my hip-hop music to help shift the narrative of invisibility.

Question: What advice would you give education practitioners who read your interview?

I want them to just listen. We have been not only silenced but erased. Till this day, there are so many kids out there that don't see themselves in the things that they love. There is a void. Sometimes you don't know there is a void until it's presented to you as a void. This happened for me when I read *America Is in the Heart* by Carlos Busolan when I was 18 in my Asian American studies course. Education practitioners need to be mindful and include access to these stories in their lesson plans. Education practitioners, the literature that we've been assigned for many years may not be right anymore. Kids today are more self-aware and their communities around them. My mom thought it was the norm to not see AAPI people in films. Only until now, does my mom know the importance of this representation after seeing and experiencing my music.

Question: Is there an Asian American ancestor that inspires you? If so, who and why?

I want to honor Dr. Dawn Mabalon. She remains one of the ancestors who inspire me to this day. Dr. Dawn Bohulano Mabalon was an American academic who worked on documenting the history of Filipino Americans. Mabalon was born in Stockton, and was the first Filipina to earn a doctoral degree in American history from Stanford University.

(Continues)

INTERVIEW WITH AMANDA PHINGBODHIPAKKIYA

Question: Who are you? What identities and intersectionalities are most salient to you today? What are you working on these days that gives you life?

I am the daughter of Thai and Indonesian immigrants. I am an artist, educator, activist, and explorer. Raised by survivors, I count myself a survivor in more ways than one. On some days, I am a warrior, and on other days, I am a healer. At times I am the one in need of healing.

I make art to invoke joy and belonging in the face of injustice, so that we might manifest futures where we are free. I create spaces for people to lay down burdens. I offer people opportunities to shed inherited narratives that no longer serve them. And I foster connection, joy, and belonging through art.

I am sandalwood, incense and lemongrass,
I am rice paddies, kelp forests and congested capitals,
I am monsoon rains and sherbert sunrises,
I am marigolds, jasmine and orchids,
I am garuda and naga,
I am sunlight glistening over crystal waters,
I am fiery woks and piercing spices,
I am bustling night markets and serene beaches,
I am banyan, pandan and eucalyptus,
I am gold splendor and gritty streets,
I am silk and sacrifice,

I am hope and hardship,
I am, like you,
Ever evolving multitudes.

Through workshops, intimate conversations and gatherings, I am building an archive of AAPI stories, histories, and dreams and inviting folks to reimagine the future with me. I believe the past can reach its hand out to remind us of who we are, where we came from, and help us understand where we're going. This archive is an offering to our communities who have so generously given the gift of their voices and visions. And every installation and experience that grows from and is shaped by this archive will hold space for our healing and restoration.

Question: What was your experience like in PK–12 education? Did you see Asian Americans reflected in the curriculum or your school?

Growing up in the American South, my formal and informal education included virtually nothing about AAPI history. Without Asian role models, I absorbed what the predominantly white culture around me told me I was — small, quiet, obedient, desired, but not respected.

I was often the only Asian kid and one of a few folks of color in my grade. It was isolating. I felt constrained, trapped, and underestimated. My classmates bullied me mercilessly for excelling at school, and for the shape of my eyes, my lunch, my differences.

I did well in STEM, which was expected, but no one expected me to love and excel in the performing arts, especially theater, a vocal extracurricular. When I was cast as the lead in the school play I remember inviting my visual arts teacher to come see me perform. After seeing the show, she seemed so utterly flabbergasted by my casting and performance: "I honestly thought you were going to be a tree in the background."

I remember one day showing my mom a recommendation letter my grade chair had written and my mom asked me pointedly: why does it say here that you're a "quiet leader." You are not quiet. In physics class one day, completely unprovoked, my teacher asked me what color I was. Even now that memory fills me with shame, shame that I did not have the courage or language to tell him how utterly wrong he was.

Question: How do you use your art as reclamation or resistance?

Art can help us hold joy and grief at the same time. When nothing else eases the pain, I always turn to art as an offering to our communities. My art helps us find peace and healing, in the face of injustice and tragedy, often through active participation.

(Continues)

(Continued)

You may have held my art at a rally or communed with me through ritual or seen my work reshape public space with warmth and care. My practice reclaims space for us in museums and galleries, on billboards, bus shelters, subway tunnels, buildings, and on the cover of *Time Magazine*.

My goal is to make work that is impossible to ignore. To create bold rebukes to hate, soaring tributes to those who have shaped us, and places of comfort and belonging. Through vibrant colors, rich patterns, and evocative imagery, they expand narratives of marginalized communities and interrogate the often unseen labor and achievement of women. My work boldly declares our belonging and pride and invites those who see it to reimagine and manifest futures we can't yet see.

Question: What advice would you give education practitioners who read your interview?

Please educate yourselves about AAPI history and ensure you're not subconsciously perpetuating harmful stereotypes about our community. During these formative years for young people, it's essential we not limit their radical imagination and exploration of identity. I want every young person to know that their voice is powerful and unique, and I want to help them find the courage to raise their voices for the causes they care about. I want them to know that there are a multitude of pathways open to them, that they can forge their own paths. And just because they behave differently from their peers, it doesn't make them less than. Our differences are often our superpowers.

Please also be conscious of holding students' multiplicities and intersectional identities. Asian American experiences are all very different. We come from all walks of life, with different traumas and treasures and lived experiences. Lumping us together creates further harm.

Please be especially aware of the fetishized sexual violence that often comes with being an Asian American girl. The ideas that have shaped these harmful behaviors have been perpetuated in the cultural consciousness for generations and have deep colonial roots. For context, the first time I experienced it, I was 12, in a mall with my mom, and a random man came up behind me and squeezed my butt, then walked away like it was nothing. People believe they have a right to Asian femme bodies. They don't. Let's arm API girls with the tools to respond and process this kind of trauma so they don't feel shame and isolation.

> # Question: Is there an Asian American ancestor that inspires you? If so, who and why?
>
> Grace Lee Boggs. She was revolutionary. She defied assumptions and stereotypes and modeled how we build intersectional arbors of cooperation across communities in powerful ways. Two of my favorite quotes from her are:
>
> > "Creativity is the key to human liberation."
> > "History is a story not only of the past but of the future."
>
> She believed deeply in the human capacity for growth and change. She championed not only protest but also reflection. I hope that I carry her spirit in my work. I certainly stand on her shoulders, as well all do.

Praxis: Action and Reflection

In this section, you will encounter two activities: one self-reflection that you can use with yourself, students, and staff, and another activity on Ekphrasis.

Activity 1: Interview Self-Reflection

After reading the two interviews from Ruby Ibarra and Amanda Phingbodhipakkiya here are few reflection questions you can use with yourself, your students, and with your staff:

◆ What are your initial takeaways from these interviews?

◆ How does identity play a role in their artform?

◆ What piece(s) of advice are you taking away from these interviews?

Activity 2: Ekphrasis: Make Art from Art from Art

Ekphrasis means "description" in Greek. Ekphrasis is a literary technique that writers use to describe a work of art, understand how a work of art impacts the writer and to inspire creativity. I'm pushing you to think of ekphrasis in a broader sense, to use art (whether visual, literary, digital, dance...etc.) to inspire more art, to build background knowledge, to provide another means for accessing content, and for reflection. So when thinking of weaving

Asian American narrative in your curriculum, you can do so through an artistic lens. Here's how to start:

1. Select a lesson in your literature or history curriculum that you want students to engage in.

2. Pick a thematic question you want your students to explore as they engage in the art pieces. For this example, I'm using the question: *"How does US imperialism and colonization impact Asian Americans?"*

3. Select and print out works of art to be placed at six different stations around the room.* Include a brief description of the work of art. For this example I'm using mainly poems and visual art pieces, but I encourage you to expand the art format by using a few multi-media stations that include podcasts, interpretive dance, music, or short films.

4. Have each student engage with each station for about 5–7 minutes.

5. Have students rotate to each station.

6. When every student has engaged in every piece of art, have students return back for more individual, small or whole group discussion revisiting the thematic question. *"How does US imperialism and colonization impact Asian Americans?"*

*For this activity, please use the work of Ruby Ibarra, Paul Tran, and Amanda Phingboddhipakkiya. Here's a quick brief outline of what to expect for each station:

PAGE #	TITLE, DESCRIPTION, AND AUTHOR
xx	"Brown Out" a rap from Ruby Ibarra about immigration
xx	"He/She" a poem from Paul Tran about gender identity and school
xx	"Very Asian Feelings" two images from Amanda Phingbodhipakkiya about Asian Americans and the American Dream
xx	"Homework" and "Snack" two poems from Amanda Phingbodhipakkiya about the American Dream and imperialism
xx	"We are More" four images from Amanda Phingbodhipakkiya about combating Asian American stereotypes and promoting belonging

You'll be surprised to see how much background knowledge this activity activates for students. I used this activity to teach about identity and intersectionality for students, parents/guardians, and teachers at the Association of Independent Schools of New England. They hired me to be the keynote speaker in 2018 for their Middle School Students of Color Conference: Living and Finessing in Color, and I offered a master class on how the arts can help us dive deeper into identity development and teach invisible narratives into visibility.

The following are two poems that accompany a series of art reflections in Figures 11.2 through 11.6 by Amanda Phingbodhipakkiya.

Station 1 Artwork: "Brown Out"

A rap by Ruby Ibarra

*They teach me to erase that brown, subconsciously I
lose my crown
'Til I don't even recognize the person that's inside me now
We came from the slums once, now livin' the humdrum
In search for the green funds, we never can keep one
My mama on 9-5, then switch to an 8-1
An immigrant family losin' our names, and our face, and
the place that we came from
These institutions working, the devil prove he lurkin'
They shoot us down but first when, we play the part
and curtains
Open up til we prefer them, 'til we don't know we hurtin'
'Til we become a version: a self that's lost it's worth
So how can I breathe in this land of the free?
My people ain't free when freedom ain't free. I look in the
mirror then all that I see
Is a version of me that they want me to be
Plus all of these lies I adopted see
I'll never be what they want me to be
The devil's at work and he lookin' like me
Can you tell me my worth? and I'll pay you the fee
'Til I fall on my knees and I'm feelin' defeat*

And so give me a reason, the image they feed
To the flows that I breathe 'cause we parted the sea
Can you pardon my speech? And the accent I speak?
I whiten my skin 'cause it's all that I see
No image of me represented to be
Myself so I'm looking for ways I could be

Station 2 Artwork: "He/She"

A poem by Paul Tran

I thought it was the wind, the Devil's Breath blowing in
from the desert, setting everything from Death Valley to the
Pacific Ocean on fire.
I thought it was the Devil: He who tried to play God.
He who cast God out of heaven
and into the sea. He who calls me out of my name
in the school bathroom, drags me by my hair into the stall
so his friends could piss on me, pull down my pants,
see what secret I tuck between my legs.
My gender has always answered
to men like him, men who make me the butt of their jokes—
the butt their toxic masculinity jerks off to—
while a urinal with "he/she" carved under my name
remains my eternal casket,
and not the principal, not the police, and not even my
mother would protest
as my attackers read my eulogy,
naming me the way colonizers name all things.
All my life, I felt the sting of men calling me a "he/she"
under my skin like the Devil's Breath,
setting everything I thought I could love about myself on fire,
and when I studied the mirror's reflection on me,
I see their lightening fists striking me again and again
and again—

These men who brag about where their dicks have been,
who grew up on the same block as me,
who stood in the same line for food stamps with me,

who share my same color and history—
I thought these men would understand
what it's like to live inside a body, I'm told, that does not
belong to me,
to have a gender as public as a bathroom,
as public as a school where we learn about the colonizers but
never the colonized:
How our ancestors kept fighting when their lands
were taken.
How they kept singing when their tongues were broken.
How they kept inventing new weapons when their minds
were chained.
How they kept rising from the flames when their loved ones
were slain.
I've lived in our colonizer's lands.
I've spoken my colonizers language,
called myself what they called me: a boy. A "he/she."
A monster.
But I'm not here to obey your binary.
I'm not here to make you comfortable.
I'm here to free myself.
I'm surrendering myself to the desert wind.
I surrender my body to fire.
I burn everything I touch
as I race to freedom.
Being genderqueer makes me nobody's son or daughter.
Being genderqueer makes me nobody's lover.
Everyone I know and love is gone.
Everyone I know and love has disowned me.
That's why I must own myself.
I own myself.
I am the sky burning red and scorched with me.
I am the sun swallowing this entire galaxy.
I am the failure of his imagination when God made me in
his image.
I am God giving himself a second chance.
I am God starting over and saying, "Let there be light,"
so these fools can see me for who I am.

FIGURE 11.2 Station 3 Artwork: "Very Asian Feelings" by Amanda Phingbodhipakkiya

FIGURE 11.3 Station 4 Artwork: "Homework" a poem by Amanda Phingboddhipakkiya

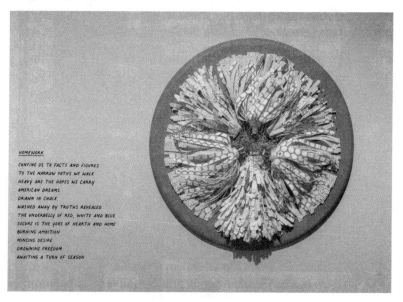

FIGURE 11.4 Station 5 Artwork: "Snack" a poem by Amanda Phingboddhipakkiya

SNACK

COMMUNION IN THE SAVORY
FALLING HEADFIRST INTO SWEET
A DIZZYING CACOPHONY OF FLAVOR
HOME
THAT FEELING ON REPEAT
TASTY'S HIDDEN MEANING
BEHIND UNWANTED GAZE
DIGNITY MADE DIRTY
UNWELCOME FINGERS TAKE
ASIAN FOODS AND BODIES
THE TASTES OF IMPERIALISM
LEAVING BRUISES
CAMOUFLAGED AS FLATTERY

A Movement, Not a Moment

There are countless resources online that talk about Asian Americans, education, and art. Another great example of an extension activity after activity 2, is to have your students write and create a Zuihitsu. The Zuihitsu is a poem that challenges the western canon because it originates from Japan. The structure of Zuihitsu is hybrid in that it can look like prose, poetry, essay, journal entry, and cataloguing and accompanies a painting that emotes similar feelings from the respective poem. I added a link to the Zuihitsu below and have compiled a few resources that I often use to help shape my own art and teaching practice more broadly:

FIGURE 11.5 Station 6 Artwork: "We are More" Protest Images by Amanda Phingboddhipakkiya

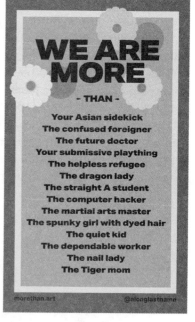

TITLE/LINK	AUTHOR(S)	WHAT'S IN THIS RESOURCE?
Margins https://aaww.org/poem-for-the-beings-who-arrived/	Marwa Helal in Asian American Writers' Workshop	This resource gives a brief description of what the Zuihitsu is and how the poet uses the form to writer about living and existing in the margins.
What it means to make Art as an Asian American in the Pandemic www.kqed.org/arts/13880441/asian-american-protest-art-pandemic	Eda Yu in KQED	This resource gives the history of Asian American social movements and the art that accompanied each movement leading up the pandemic.
Inventing a Culture: Asian American Poetry in the 1970s shc.stanford.edu/arcade/interventions/inventing-culture-asian-american-poetry-1970s	Timothy Yu in *Locating Contemporary Asian American Poetry* (Stanford University)	This resource describes how Asian American poetry in the 1970's was an avant-garde through content, style and structure of writing.
What We Look Like www.nytimes.com/2020/06/06/us/coronavirus-race-artists-asian-american-identity.html	Antonio de Luca and Jaspal Riyait in *The New York Times*	This resource includes 11 Asian American artists that showcase a self-portrait that explores what it means to be Asian American.

Chapter 12

Teaching Asian American Studies Through Pop Culture

LEARNING OBJECTIVES:

◆ Practitioners will learn how pop culture is a portal to Asian American history past, present, and future (knowledge).

◆ Practitioners will learn how Asian American pop culture resonates with youth (knowledge and mindset).

◆ Practitioners will learn how to teach Asian American studies through pop culture (skill).

The Personal Is Political

"Shut up, I can beat you up! I'm serious..."

Michelle Yeoh says this remark in her 2023 Golden Globe speech for winning Best Actress in *Everything Everywhere All At Once* as she responded to the exit music that attempted to shrink her legendary moment. Of course she meant this in the comical sense of her being fluent in martial arts. I start this chapter with this historical moment, because it speaks to many different concepts in this book. First, it speaks to the intersectionality and intergenerationality of Asian American women in film and the future. She is a Chinese and Malaysian, she is a woman, and she is in her 60s, and when do we ever get to see magic take up so much space in the media with this combination of identities? Right, never.

The media industry is entrenched in white dominance. Like the Golden Globes, the Oscars have too been criticized for its white dominance. If you Google the term #OscarsSoWhite you will find yourself in a labyrinth of resources pointing to why and how the Oscars (and other media platforms) are so white and why Asian Americans have been shuffled to the margins or merely omitted from roles that were designed for Asian Americans. So with regard to the future, pop culture is a portal to seeing Asian Americans beyond the past, beyond the white gaze, and Michelle Yeoh has just stretched the portal wider for more Asian Americans to enter and center themselves.

Yeoh's quip combats the model minority myth because it paints the counter-story of Asian Americans and Asian American women as confident, powerful, and resistant. In a recent NBC Asian America interview (Yam, 2023) with the author of *Asian American Histories of the United States*, Dr. Catherine Ceniza Choy states: "We have to live with these stereotypes and expectations of being demure and diminutive on the daily. So to witness that on such a big stage of something like the Golden Globes was profound."

Another piece that Yeoh embodies is this concept of Asian Americans exhibiting humor. She uses sarcasm in her own immigration story of experiencing the perpetual foreigner stereotype hearing a white person say, "You speak English," with Yeoh responding, "The flight was 13 hours long, so I learned," while the crowd laughs with her as she pokes at the model minority myth. Above all, this moment in pop culture shows how Asian American women can embody the multiplicity of identities balancing regality with humor, graciousness with pride, and confidence with humbleness.

Lastly, Yeoh pays homage to those who have come before, which is a very Asian American concept of honoring our ancestors with the statement, "This is also for all the shoulders that I stand on, all who came before me, who look like me and all who are going on this journey with me forward." This analysis came out of a three minute speech and moment of resistance and Asian American joy.

After reading many analyses of Yeoh's moment, one stood out to me because it focuses on the image of the camera panning toward a younger actress Stephanie Hsu as Michelle Yeoh speaks. Yeong Cheng (they/them), a DEI strategist and friend, shared a reflection on LinkedIn on what Stephanie Hsu's facial expression could symbolize to the rest of the Asian American community:

"This is the face of a human being coping with the dissolution of the binaries in which they were placed from birth. It's the face people make when our intellectual understanding of our personhood becomes somatic. It's the face of expanded possibilities. It's the face of "I can do that." It's the face of "If I can do that, what else can I do?" It's the face of "Who would I be today if I had grown up seeing this?"

This anaphoric reflection could not be more salient. Seeing Hsu's authentic tears of joy can make any of us Asian Americans tear up as well. It can feel somatic even through a computer screen, which illuminates how powerful this moment is.

Like Hsu's reaction, in this chapter, you'll learn about my earliest connections to Asian American pop culture. Then you'll learn from another Asian American Avenger, Richard Leong, and his story and recommendations on how to include Asian American pop culture in schools.

Earliest Messages of Asian American Pop Culture

My first experience with Asian Americans and pop culture was seeing Dante Basco play Rufio in the 1991 Steven Spielberg movie *Hook*. I can't tell you how many times I watched and continue to watch this classic. Like Yeoh, Rufio is another symbol of Asian Americans that resisted the model minority stereotype. Rufio was the leader of The Lost Boys, a ragtag crew of youth who refused to grow up, fought against pirates, and lived in Neverland.

Seeing Rufio played by a Filipino American was an incredible moment. When you first get introduced to Rufio, he comes in with a skateboard, clad in all black, with a tri-hawk with red streaks, while The Lost Boys chant his name like Hercules. You cannot watch this entrance scene and not think to yourself, "Well damn, he's the coolest character in this entire movie." Steven Spielberg admitted too in an interview that he hired Dante Basco, because he scared the shit out of him. You have to laugh. Rufio was clearly not your average Asian American.

In high school, I later used Rufio as a nickname while competing in sports, and soon it stuck and followed me throughout my entire high school experience. I even dressed up as Rufio for Halloween and became one of the coolest kids in a school that was 99 percent white. Before using the name Rufio, this Asian American boy was invisible, meek, and living under my sister's shadow. Rufio opened up a portal.

After changing my name to Rufio, everyone at my school seemed to be able to connect because of the zeitgeist of *Hook*. I had more confidence in myself and extended myself to so many different extracurricular activities. I spoke up more in class. I even got named Homecoming Prince. How did this all happen? Rufio's name and Dante's representation for a young Filipino American like myself growing up in rural Ohio was transformational. This is the power of representation in film and what it can mean to both Asian American and non–Asian American kids in education. Rufio gave us a common language. Rufio was radical imagination, stretching everyone's expectations for what a 5 foot 8 Asian American kid could actually be.

REFLECTION QUESTION

When you see Asian American students, staff members or community member, what are the first depictions that come to mind? Do you see Michelle Yeoh or Dante Basco? Or do you see the typical model minority? Why or Why not?

Asian American Pop Culture Today and Education

One fun fact about Dante Basco is that in 2020 at the height of the #StopAsianHate movement, I had the opportunity to speak on a panel with him through FilAm Arts. Talk about a dream come true!

At this event, I also met Richard Leong, a fellow disruptive educator, DEI strategist, and advocate for using Asian American pop culture in education. In the next section, you will learn more about his story and strategies on how to incorporate Asian American pop culture in your school.

Praxis: Action and Reflection

CONVERSATION WITH RICHARD LEONG, A DISRUPTIVE EDUCATOR AND DEI STRATEGIST

Hi Richard! Can you introduce yourself to our readers?

Hi folks, my name is Richard Leong, my pronouns are he/him, and I'm a DEI consultant and facilitator. I spend most of my time thinking about how to build systems oriented around fairness and equity at work and in life. I used to be a fifth grade teacher working in a predominantly Hmong community of St. Paul, MN, and it was during those years that I really started thinking about how I could incorporate Asian American pop culture into my classroom.

To really understand my story, I think you have to know the complexity of the layers to my identities. My parents are immigrants from Hong Kong and Taiwan who met in Los Angeles in 1984, but by the time I was born in 1992 our family was part of the American expat community in Beijing. Because we spoke English at home and I went to international school where classes were taught in English, I craved English entertainment, but the only English programming available on TV was CNN.

You have no idea how happy I was when we finally moved (back) to America. All of a sudden, Pokemon was on TV, and I didn't have to hunt through flea markets looking for VHS tapes in English. Not only Pokemon, but I soon discovered Digimon, Dragonball Z, Yu-Gi-Oh — a whole world of

(Continues)

(Continued)

Japanese anime available in English to fill my weekday nights and Saturday mornings. I share this story because I think all of us, even as children, look for entertainment that we see ourselves in. I didn't really think consciously about race or ethnicity, but like me Ash Ketchum ate rice and noodles, had black hair that stuck out in weird angles when it wasn't covered by a hat, and he dreamt big about traveling the world with his friends. I didn't realize it at the time, but looking back, I never watched a lot of American shows as a kid because the dubbed anime content that made it over felt distinctively Asian and connected with me in a way that mainstream content on Nickelodeon and Cartoon Network didn't.

Can you tell us why pop culture can be a useful tool in the classroom for teaching Asian American history or culture?

The biggest reason is that it's fun! We all know our students are connecting every day on the sports, music, and entertainment that is popular to them. In many ways the integration of pop culture into the classroom is just about meeting our students where they're at. Leveraging pop culture in the classroom allows for the following:

-For you to share what aspects of Asian American pop culture you have encountered and what resonates with you and why?

-To literary techniques and to access student emotions. For example, I think about the lyrics of Olivia Rodrigo's "good 4 u" and think about the literary techniques of irony and sarcasm, while tapping into the pain of a teenage break up.

Can you share an example of how you've used pop culture to explore the Asian American experience?

In 2021 when *Shang-Chi and the Legend of the Ten Rings* came out, I was such a fan I went to see it multiple times in theaters. I have to give full credit to my friend and fellow Asian American former teacher-now-DEI consultant Joyce Chiao for this because she texted me right as I was getting on a plane from LAX to Boston asking if I'd be interested in working with her to write a set of discussion questions and curate a set of additional resources to help other Asian Americans process and make meaning of the movie. By the end of that five and half hour flight, I had my first draft of questions done.

In our Shang-Chi Syllabus and Discussion Guide, we divided our questions by topic, focusing on using the film as a starting point for deeper explorations of Asian American experiences and representation. For example, we asked folks to think about how the women characters relate to gender norms surrounding Asian women, and the history of their portrayal in Western cinema. Because much of the film's dialogue was in Mandarin, we asked our readers to consider how one's language connects to identity. Family is a deeply important theme in the movie, and we asked readers to think about what family dynamics in the film they might or might not identify with in their own lived experiences.

Thinking about our readers, what are some strategies that teachers can use to integrate Asian American pop culture into their lesson plans?

Here are a couple of reflection questions that can help guide you toward a meaningful lesson.

What are your students into? What excites them and what do they enjoy talking about? If you don't know, just ask!

What challenges do the Asian and Asian American students in your classroom face in your local context? What barriers do your school support staff and community leaders support your families in navigating?

How will you equip your students with the tools and vocabulary to engage in critical thinking about the media they engage with? Consider leveraging tools from the world of media literacy, and partner with your colleagues in creative/musical arts.

How will you prepare for nuanced and complex conversation about Asian American experiences, if you do not identify as Asian? What are helpful ways for you to learn about Asian American history, and who are leaders in the community you can invite into the classroom?

Let's go deeper into the Shang-Chi syllabus. Here are a few topics and discussion questions that teachers can dive into after watching the movie with their students:

Family Dynamics

◆ How would you describe Shang-Chi's relationship with his father at the start of the film, and how does it change by the end? How does this relationship drive Shang-Chi's character development?

◆ Much of the plot is driven by Xu Wenwu grappling with grief over the loss of his wife, Ying Li. How do the other Xu family members process their grief, and how does that affect their relationships with one another? Does the family ever experience healing?

◆ Sacrifice is an unspoken expression of love for the Xu family. How does sacrifice, from Shang-Chi and others in his family, influence the way that Shang-Chi understands his relationships to his family? How does sacrifice shift Shang-Chi's relationship to his family throughout the film?

Gender Roles

◆ There is a history of desexualization and the emasculation of Asian men when represented in Western media. In a scene at the Golden Daggers, Katy reacts with surprise to Shang-Chi's shirtless torso. Given this context, what was your reaction to this scene? Did you find Shang-Chi "sexy" or attractive in a conventional way?

◆ How do the characters of Xialing, Katy, and Ying Nan relate to the gender norms often surrounding Asian women? In what ways do they conform to, debunk, or add nuance to traditional norms?

◆ What role does Ying Li's presence and absence throughout the movie play in character development for the rest of the Xu family? In what ways does this dynamic tell a larger story about the family's collective relationship to the mother?

Language

◆ Much of the dialogue in this film was in Mandarin, with almost 20 minutes elapsing before English was heard in the film — a rarity for a film made by an American studio. How did you experience the use of Mandarin and English dialogue throughout the movie? What dynamic did that have on your experience of watching the film?

◆ If you understand Mandarin, you may have noticed several moments where the subtitles differed from what was spoken by the characters. Did any moments jump out to you? Why might the movie have used these alterations? Do you agree or disagree with this approach? Why?

◆ When Shang-Chi and Katy arrive in Macau, the difference between their knowledge of Mandarin is emphasized in their interaction with Jon Jon played by Ronny Chieng. When Katy shares that she doesn't speak Chinese, Jon Jon replies, "It's all good. I speak ABC," which in this context has a dual meaning as both English and "American-born Chinese." What do you make of this scene, and how does it illustrate a connection between identity and language?

A Movement, Not a Moment

Hearing from Richard and myself are but windows into how we can leverage pop culture to teach Asian American studies and histories. I can't help but think how similar our experiences are even if his family is from Hong Kong and Taiwan. That's the beauty of diasporic stories, you never know where bridges can be built. The way Richard and Joyce designed the questions for the Shang-Chi syllabus makes it easy for high school teachers to leverage right after watching the video. There is so much beyond family dynamics, gender roles, and language that could be explored with your class. Of course, for upper elementary through middle school teachers, depending on your students grade level, you might have to adapt the questions to meet your classroom needs.

After this chapter, I encourage you to revisit the Shang-Chi syllabus, as well as engage in the following resources that I often reference when teaching Asian American pop culture and its impacts on the United States:

TITLE/LINK	AUTHOR(S)	WHAT'S IN THIS RESOURCE?
We Are Here: Stories from 30 Inspiring Asian American and Pacific Islanders Who have Shaped the United States learninglab.si.edu/org/apac	Smithsonian Asian Pacific American Center	This resource provides access to objects, works of art, videos, archival materials, and websites that expand each person's biography in We Are Here.
RISE: A Pop History of Asian America from the Nineties to Now www.harpercollins.com/pages/Rise	Jeff Yang, Phil Yu, and Philip Wang	This resource includes the voices, emotions, and memories of Asian Americans that shaped pop culture from the 90's to now.

(Continues)

(Continued)

Title/Link	Author(s)	What's in This Resource?
How Asian Americans have Influenced Popular Culture now.tufts.edu/2022/05/18/how-asian-americans-have-influenced-popular-culture	Monica Jimenez in Tufts Now	This resource includes an interview on the intersections of Asian America and Pop Culture featuring Tasha Oren (Director of Film and Media Studies at Tufts University).
Reappropriate reappropriate.co	Jenn Fang	This resource is one of the web's oldest Asian American blogs that focuses on feminism, politics, and pop culture.
Shang-Chi: Syllabus and Discussion Guide	Joyce Chiao and Richard Leong	This is Joyce and Richard's fan-made set of questions and resources to help make deeper meaning of Shang-Chi.
Asians in Hollywood	Accented Cinema	Accented Cinema is a fantastic YouTube account with critical analyses of multiple movies, including Asian and Asian American content. This video is an overview of Asians in western media, and while I don't agree with everything in it, it's a useful resource for those looking for an overview.
The Prevalence and Portrayal of Asian and Pacific Islanders across 1300 Popular Films	Dr. Nancy Wang Yuen, Dr. Stacy L. Smith, Dr. Katherine Pieper, Marc Choueiti, Kevin Yao, and Dana Dinh	There are lots of graphs and data here that relate to the disparity in roles and representation not just for API folks broadly, but the various ethnicities within the API community.

Part 4

Teach Us Visible by Moving with Us

Chapter 13

Working with Asian American Students, Staff, and Families

LEARNING OBJECTIVES:

◆ Practitioners will shift their understanding of curriculum (mindset).

◆ Practitioners will learn how to work with Asian American students, staff, and communities (skill).

The Personal Is Political

"When you teach, half of the curriculum walks into your classroom."

While working with Dr. Josephine Kim at the Harvard Graduate School of Education teaching Asian American studies in 2021, she told me that scholar Emily Styles argues that you can only lesson plan so far in advance, because half of your curriculum is brought in by your students. Basically, she expands our common definitions of "curriculum." Curriculum is normally seen as the scope-in-sequence that we develop and parse out into individual lesson plans. Nowhere in my teacher training did anyone say that curriculum could also (and should also) be defined as the students you work with. That shift in definition and mindset helps you center and consider the concept of culture that often gets missed in teaching students of color.

If we think about culturally responsive and sustaining teaching practices (CRST), there is a limit to how much we can plan for our students until we actually learn who they are. Specifically, Asian American youth and their culture often get overlooked when teachers employ CRST strategies because the model minority posits that they don't need CRST. Regrettably, I did two things that were harmful toward my Asian American students:

♦ I saw them through the model minority frame, which hindered me from understanding who they were.

♦ When I did employ CRST practices toward Asian American youth they were haphazard and inconsistent.

Dr. Gloria Ladson-Billings references this concept of overlooking Asian American students in *The Dreamkeepers*. She gives the example of a student who often gets pushed into the advanced placement, when in reality, they needed and preferred that English Language Learning environment in which they were originally placed.

REFLECTION QUESTIONS

Have you ever worked with an Asian American student population? If so, were they the minority or majority?

Have you ever applied the model minority stereotype toward your students? (This can be Asian American or other groups that suffer from this stereotype .) If so, what would you do differently to change the approach?

Zooming out, this makes me think about how non–Asian American education practitioners approach Asian American students, staff, and family members. The model minority myth homogenizes the Asian American community, while saying that "Asian Americans are doing just fine." This renders us passive subjects in a classroom.

With regard to research, the data around Asian Americans and school say otherwise. If we look at the number of high school diplomas across historically marginalized Asian Americans in education, you'll see from the United States Census and Department of Commerce report in 2014 shared on the TFA AAPI website, the following percentages of students from the following groups achieved a high school diploma:

♦ 50% Bhutanese

♦ 62% Hmong and Cambodian

♦ 66% Laotian

♦ 71% Vietnamese, Tongan, and Melanesian American

♦ 72% Burmese

On top of that, it would be foolish to think that any other Asian American group that are not on this list are doing "OK." This is just an example of the *invisible within the invisible*.

Since I have been a student, teacher, and now a parent at a school, I have experienced a pattern of interactions that intersect common stereotypes that stem from the model minority myth or the perpetual foreigner concept. Arguably, because I have experienced them, I've also perpetuated them. This chapter aims at highlighting the unspoken concepts to think about when approaching Asian Americans in your school at all levels. This will require you to revisit Chapter 2 on Windows, Mirror, and Sliding Glass doors. How we are racialized and socialized informs the way we approach Asian Americans in education. In the Praxis section, you'll learn what to consider when working with us at all levels.

Praxis: Action and Reflection

Let me reiterate the statement, "Asian Americans are the fastest growing racial group in the country," according to Pew Research. As our schools begin to usher in more Asian Americans, we need to discuss how to work with our students, staff members, and families. For this reason, I've invited my friend Alice Tsui (pronounced "Tsoy"), a Grammy-nominated music educator in Brooklyn, to co-write and share wisdom throughout this section. You'll know when one of us is speaking because you'll see our name next to the section title.

Student Level

Here are some student-level activities.

COMBAT THE CROSS-RACE EFFECT (TONY)

Asian Americans often hear the phrase from non-Asians that "all Asians look the same." It's incredibly biased and flattening. This is commonly called the "cross-race effect" or "own-race bias." The cross-race effect (CRE) in memory refers to the well-replicated finding that humans are better at remembering faces from their own racial group, relative to other groups (Malpass & Kravitz, 1969). This may seem harmless, but it often leads to the misidentification of people of color.

You combat cross-race effect by:

◆ Practicing recognizing facial characteristics of Asian Americans through more exposure to our culture

◆ Not confusing one Asian American person for another

◆ Not assuming that Asian Americans are all related

NAME PRONUNCIATION (ALICE)

This should go without saying, but pronouncing each person's name accurately as the person who is the holder of that name pronounces it is necessary. Throughout my life, my own last name Tsui, has been and continues to be mispronounced and made fun of. There are a multitude of stories and pop culture instances in which Asian names are ridiculed. Each name carries a story, a history, and a pathway to understanding. There is no such thing as a name that is too difficult to pronounce. You can consider how you can improve your own pronunciation of Asian names by:

◆ Listening intently to students, colleagues, and community members when they first introduce themselves.

◆ Repeat the name aloud.

◆ Ask the person to pronounce it again if necessary.

◆ Thank each person for sharing their pronunciation.

◆ Practice on your own time.

◆ If you overhear a student, colleague, or community member mispronouncing a name, step in and correct them.

OPPORTUNITIES TO SPEAK (TONY)

Asian American students who are not the majority rarely get opportunities to speak and give feedback. Part of the model minority myth assumes that we are quiet and humble, which can relate to us not participating in class or being outspoken. I know I internalized this up until late high school. I conflated speaking with taking up too much space and being annoying. But speaking helps us get better at oral communication in public spaces, which is an essential skill in the 21st century.

Some ways to build more opportunities in class to speak are:

◆ Building in time for small groups and giving roles that transition. This can be intentional think pair shares and/or groups of four with transitioning tasks that force students to do low-stakes speaking like reading aloud or having them share what their partner said in conversation.

◆ Keep a tracker of who speaks and who doesn't in class. This is something I did to track youth voice. In every school I taught at and served as an instructional coach where Asian Americans were the minority, they would speak the least unless intentionally invited to speak through warm-calling. Warm-calling is different than "cold-calling" because it invites students to speak, and allows them permission to decline as to not build harmful stress or anxiety. This practice can help you build equity of voice in the class.

◆ Assign a public speaking presentation and ask what support your Asian American student needs in a one-on-one meeting. When I taught in Jamaica Plain, MA, I taught a Vietnamese student Bao Nghi, and while she didn't speak often, it didn't mean she couldn't. For one of our assignments, I gave her a performance poem to present that she wrote or one she selected to be her favorite during April's National Poetry Month. She rose to the challenge, memorized a poem, and performed it.

INTENTIONAL LISTENING (ALICE)

We can advocate for and support Asian American students, educators, and families by considering our own intentional listening. Parent teacher conferences are an example of a crucial and often stressful time for students and families due to academic stresses, potential language barriers, and educational differences. Intentionally listen to:

◆ What the adults in the family are sharing as you are speaking to them

◆ What the Asian American child is saying in return if they are translating for their family member(s)

◆ The silences that may occur within the conversation, without feeling the need to fill each one

OPPORTUNITIES TO LEAD (TONY)

Asian Americans often face our version of the glass ceiling in leadership referred to as "the bamboo ceiling." This is caused when people don't think of us as leadership material. The model minority myth is another way that suppresses our image. How many Asian American CEOs can you name on one hand? Right, that is not something that first comes to mind.

We combat this by paying attention to the assets that Asian American students bring to the classroom. Activist Adrienne Maree Brown says, "what you pay attention to grows," so pay attention to what Asian American students bring to the table. Leadership in the classroom can look like students helping out with small or large tasks. It can look like students leading a warm up or end of class activity. It can even look like students teaching the class a short lesson.

CONSENT ABOUT SHARING LIVED EXPERIENCE IN WHOLE GROUP (TONY)

One example of consent in teaching is not to force students to speak for the entire Asian American community. Teachers do this without even thinking, especially when they have that one Asian American student or student of color and they are trying to make a recent connection to worldly events that may involve their racial group. For example, I have had teachers call on me to speak on the Bataan Death March, when I have no recollection of what that was or connection to that traumatic event. When I coached teachers, I saw teachers pan their eyes toward the one Asian student multiple times and for extended periods of time expecting a response from them. It's important to know that our Asian American students don't all come from cultures that expect them to speak or actively engage the way we may define engagement, which is why it's an important practice to co-define this together. Some ways to combat the somatic impulse to cold-call or harmfully spotlight an Asian American student are the following:

♦ When referencing anything about Asian America, don't look or pan to the Asian American identifying student, especially if it makes them uncomfortable.

♦ If you think you are about to talk about Asian American narratives in a future lesson, ask for consent by talking with the student individually if they feel like they want to share or contribute. If they do want to share, then you just learned how to prepare them. If they don't want to share, then you can prepare yourself to handle potential moments when students pan their eyes toward the one Asian American student when Asian American content is being discussed.

ETHNORACIAL MATCHING (TONY)

Ethnoracial matching is when administrators hire and place teachers with students that share a similar or same ethnic or racial identity. Studies have shown that this increases retention of Black students. A recent study shows that matching helps with lowering discipline issues with Asian American students. Imagine we hire more Asian American teachers and match them with Asian American students; there may be a positive effect on behavior and creating a sense of well-being and belonging.

To add more nuance and to combat the idea that all "Asians are the same," we cannot expect someone who is Japanese American to have the same impacts on Vietnamese newcomers. While there are overlaps in racialized experiences, the two cultures are very different and distinct. Matching Vietnamese newcomers with Vietnamese teachers may be a stronger fit, and again this all depends on whether the Vietnamese teacher has a strong sense of identity development.

Staff Level

Here are some activities for the staff.

SEE ASIAN AMERICANS AS PEOPLE OF COLOR (TONY)

Believe it or not, while this seems obvious, teaching people that Asian Americans are people of color is an issue today. This model minority myth has been used to create an image of Asian Americans as white-adjacent, "honorary white," or even white, depending on who you talk to and what piece of data informs your definition of "white."

If we look at national household median income, according to the National Community Reinvestment Coalition and the United States Census, the household median income for Asian Americans increased by 4.6 percent from 2017 to $87,194 in 2018, 38 percent greater than the national median income of $63,179. Based on this statistic, I can see why people might conclude that Asian Americans can be compared to white households. However, this does not account for the amount of people who live, on average, in Asian households or which Asian Americans we are talking about. In 2017, Asian Americans on average had a household size of 3.04, compared to the national average of 2.65.

Additionally, Asian Americans disproportionately live in metropolitan areas where the cost of living is high, such as Los Angeles, San Francisco, and New York City. If we disaggregate the data, you will notice that the Burmese American population had an average median household income of $36,000, way below the poverty line. We have to consider these factors to understand the story behind the data and how this informs how people view and characterize Asian Americans.

According to a 2022 STAATUS Index report, the majority of Asian Americans do not identify as white, nor do they perceive their status as white adjacent. Rather, 63 percent of Asian Americans identify as a person of color, and 76 percent perceive their status as closer to people of color than to whites. In addition, the majority of Black Americans (63 percent) and Hispanic Americans (56 percent) also perceive Asian Americans as closer to people of color than to white Americans. By stark contrast, 69 percent of white Americans perceive the status of Asian Americans as closer to white people, pointing to a disjuncture in the way that white Americans perceive Asians compared to all other groups, including Asian Americans.

The best ways to combat the narrative that Asians are not people of color is to do the following:

♦ Disaggregate student and staff data for Asian Americans by ethnicity, and while you're at it, every other group. This will help you compare how the different intersections of identity can lead to different education outcomes at school.

♦ Learn the history of Asian Americans and the fight for ethnic studies. This call to action is a reminder from my chapter on teaching Asian American cross-racial narratives. The movement for ethnic studies was co-led by Asian Americans fighting for space in professional white institutions (PWIs).

♦ Educate yourself on topics regarding the concept of "Asians as People of Color." In 2018, my colleagues and I curated a panel of education practitioners and scholars that talks directly to these experiences as seen in the image below (see Figure 13.1). Learn more by visiting: bit.ly/AreAsiansPOC (case sensitive).

FIGURE 13.1   Tony DelaRosa facilitating the panel "Are Asians People of Color?" panel at Harvard Graduate School of Education in 2018

Affinity Spaces (Tony)

Any racial group can benefit from having a psychological safe space to be their authentic selves. I find that affinity spaces for people of color, and even more specifically, for Asian Americans have been very helpful for my own well-being and sense of belonging. One example of this type of program is the Asian American Teaching Empowerment, Networking, and Development Initiative (AATEND). I co-founded this program with Richard Haynes, the Director of School Support at NYC Men Teach in 2020. It is a part of a broader initiative by the New York City Mayor's office of recruiting and supporting 1,000 male teachers of color in NYC.

The AATEND program is important to me because this is one of the first I've encountered that specifically focuses on Asian American educators who identify as men. This program allows for nuanced support reckoning with both toxic masculinity and being stereotyped as effeminate, understanding and actualizing our fight against anti-Blackness, and breaking the bamboo ceiling. If your school has any Asian American staff members, work with them to see if an affinity space would benefit them. Depending on the number of Asian Americans, we may want to aggregate up to a larger people of color affinity space if we don't have a lot of representation in the school. I encourage teachers to replicate this at their schools if there is enough racial affinity across staff that feels substantive. If there is no substantive racial diversity at your school that shares your racial affinity, then I encourage teachers and administrators to reach out to their districts to find ways to do this across schools, which can potentially combine budgets for support.

Once the affinity space is created, ask what type of budget they may need to sustain themselves at work. Sustaining oneself can mean hosting internal programming for fellow Asian American staff members or finding time to commiserate over a meal. Many Asian American affinity spaces have used the intersection of food and education as a low lift strategy to come together, build community, strengthen collective identity, and celebrate the similarities and differences within the Asian diaspora.

Opportunities to Lead (Tony)

One of the reasons why I started the NYC Men Teach AATEND program was to help Asian American teachers ascend into education leadership positions. We have done that internally by training Asian American male teachers through project management and leadership coaching. According to the United States Census, 79 percent of our teachers are white, but nearly 50 percent of K–12 public school students are Black, Asian American, Hispanic, Native American, and Pacific Islander. According to the National Center of Education Statistics, Asian American teachers make up 2 percent of our public-school teachers, while Asian American students make up around 5 percent and with the population growing, this will increase. Asian Americans comprise .9 percent of public schools and 1.9 percent of private schools according to the National Center of Education Statistics.

Part of wanting to be a leader is having this representation in the building. Beyond ethnoracial matching as mentioned as a strategy to help Asian American students, I want to see more Asian Americans in PK–12 leadership because it also shows to non–Asian Americans that we have leadership potential, which can change the narrative around Asians in education. Currently, "less than 2% of PK–12 principals are from Asian American and Pacific Islander backgrounds. Teachers who identify as AAPI represent a little over 2.5% of the teaching workforce in public schools," according to Education Week reporter Denisa R. Superville (2023).

Family Level (Tony)

When you Google "Asian American parents" you will see within the top 10 searches anything from these words or phrases: "harsh parenting," "discard old stereotypes," " parenting and Mental Health," "focus on parenting," and "strong-minded parenting." If you were to read this and make a snap judgment about our parents, what would you think? This might lead people to the stereotype of a "Tiger Parent," this idea that Asian American parents have a strong will, place immense value on education, and are harsh in accountability.

In my own Asian American friend circles, joking about the "Tiger Parent" can seem common across the diaspora because many of us have experienced this type of parenting. But like all stereotypes, they are stories that are only half true. As you think about being pro–Asian American in your approach to working with us, I say "us" now because I recently became a parent, I want you to consider the following.

Not Every Asian Parent Is a Tiger Parent (Tony)

To assume that every Asian American parent is a Tiger Parent is flattening and racially biased. I have seen teachers treat Asian parents with more positive regard than other students of color because of the perceived emphasis on education. This can be damaging, because back to Dr. Gloria Ladson-Billings point in *The Dreamkeepers*, we can get easily swept away in applying the model minority myth as it comes to the types of resources we think Asian American families have.

Respecting Both Immediate and Extended Family Members (Tony)

As referenced above, many Asian American households have extended family living in the same household. This is a hallmark of many Asian cultures that value collectivism over individualism, which manifests as families being extremely tight-knit. In Filipino culture, we call these households "compounds," where multiple families live together for mutual support. So it is not unheard of for another family member to arrive at the quarterly "parent teacher conference." Being pro–Asian American means you are extending the level of respect from the immediate family to the extended family as well. From an administrative standpoint, this can be an opportunity to collect information from Asian American students on who may be the multiple points of contact.

Provide Opportunities to Share About Difference in Asian and US School Systems (Tony)

Depending on the family, you may have Asian American parents who have had a different education experience than the one you are providing their children. This is especially true if the parent identifies as a refugee or recent immigrant. Remember that Asia is humongous, so even across Asia, the education experience is different. While middle-high income families from somewhere like Japan emphasize after-school tutoring due to the concept of *juku,* or cram school, to help prepare for summative assessments, other families may not have this emphasis due to access. In urban school districts in the Philippines, schools are so overcrowded that students have to take shifts when they are allowed to attend school. These two different experiences can shape how Asian American parents view and approach education for their children.

A Movement, Not a Moment

You just learned about different considerations and approaches when working with Asian American students, staff members, and families. One theme rings true throughout all stakeholder levels; consent in your approach to the Asian American community is key. The following is a list of resources that will help you strengthen your pro–Asian American lens when working with us:

TITLE/LINK	AUTHOR(S)	WHAT'S IN THIS RESOURCE?
How Teachers Can Break Down Stereotypes of Asian American Students www.edweek.org/leadership/how-teachers-can-break-down-stereotypes-of-asian-american-students/2022/10	Ileanna Najarro in *Education Week*	This resource offers interventions on how to approach Asian American students.
Educators Making a Difference: Building Affinity Spaces for Asian American Teachers smithsonianapa.org/learn/learn-archives/affinity-spaces/	Tony DelaRosa in *Smithsonian Asian Pacific American Center*	This resource is an interview that showcases ways to build an Asian American affinity space at your school.
What is Tiger Parenting, and How does it affect children? www.apadivisions.org/division-7/publications/newsletters/developmental/2013/07/tiger-parenting	Su Yeong Kim in *Developmental Psychologist Summer 2013*	This resource defines the term "Tiger Parent." It showcases the perspective of Asian American parents, researchers, and the importance of studying this concept.

(Continues)

(Continued)

Title/Link	Author(s)	What's in This Resource?
Working with Asian Parents and Families www.proquest.com/ openview/61bcec116 4887fa73cc2cd6e4af82e16/ 1?cbl=33246&pq-origsite=gscholar	Guang-Lea Lee & M. Lee Manning in *Promising Practices 2001*	This resource gives tangible advice on what to consider when working with Asian American parents and families.
Racial Wealth Snapshot: Asian Americans and the racial wealth divide ncrc.org/racial-wealth-snapshot-asian-americans-and-the-racial-wealth-divide/#_ftn8	Dedrick Asante-Muhammad and Sally Sim in *National Community Reinvestment Coalition*	This resource breaks down where Asian Americans fall in the racial wealth divide. It disaggregates data by wealth, ethnicity, education, and more.

Chapter 14

Combating Anti-Asian Hate Case Study Workshop

LEARNING OBJECTIVES:

- ◆ Practitioners will learn how to identify anti-Asian hate, violence, and racism that may arise in schools through practice (skill).

- ◆ Practitioners will learn how to reflect and respond in the moment when they encounter anti-Asian hate, violence, and racism (skill).

The Personal Is Political

"Stop gaslighting Asians for speaking up about Anti-Asian racism."

I'm quoting SegregAsian, which was formerly an organization that posted about Asian American education and politics on Instagram. Yes, Instagram. Believe it or not, Instagram is where I turned to when trying to learn more about issues that impact the Asian American community. I posted that quote on my own Instagram page @TonyRosaSpeaks, on August 21, 2020. This is the year of the rise of anti-Asian hate and racism. In the summer I was working as a diversity, equity, and inclusion facilitator (DEIF) for a large organization that places teachers in historically and systemically underserved schools. My role as a DEIF was to train pre-service teachers in how to embody DEI through teaching.

That same year I learned of the term "gaslighting," which means to "manipulate (someone) using psychological methods into questioning their own sanity or powers of reasoning" (Oxford Dictionary). The term "manipulation" sounds active, but in my own experience as a DEIF, I've understood it to be both active and passive.

That summer of 2020, I fought hard to include lessons and strategies on how to combat anti-Asian violence in the curriculum that would build the anti-racist knowledge, skills, mindsets, and ways of being for new teachers all over the United States. If we are going to be "aspiring anti-racist educators," we must think and act in a cross-coalitional and intersectional frame lest we cheapen the meaning and water down the impact of collective liberation. Despite my advocacy to senior leaders, my suggestions were omitted, which is another form of gaslighting. To me "omission" is active, but sounds passive or like an accident. But what does this say about how we view Asian American children and staff members in our US education system? Omitting this topic in national education curriculum does the following:

◆ Shows that most educators still view Asian Americans as a monolith while some of the most marginalized Asian American communities in the United States get further erased.

◆ Shows that Asian Americans are not a part of or deserving of collective liberation but our labor is still required.

◆ Says that Asians don't experience racism.

◆ It upholds the Black-white binary that is the United States education system.

◆ It upholds white supremacy because at the end of the day it wanted Asian Americans to be quiet, submissive, complicit, anti-Black, to be the "good immigrant," to be pro-nationalist.

I posted this commentary on Instagram, which soon took off with engagement. People, especially Asian Americans, felt this statement, which is why I include the story and this case study analysis activity here for practitioners. I include it as one of the last chapters of this book because I want us to depart with the urgency to practice how to become pro–Asian American in schools. Anti-bias and anti-racist work is somatic; it has to live in the body in order for it to become a habit. We can host book clubs upon book clubs, but in all honesty that is only step one. Allyship is a verb. No matter how many training sessions I have led on anti-bias and anti-racism, I still make it a point to attend training, even if it means to practice.

Praxis: Action and Reflection

In this section, you will read six case studies that intersect anti-Asian hate, violence, and racism. These case studies can be used to train ourselves as practitioners in PK–12 schools.

Before you begin, I always start this training with community principles, as you can see. To save time and after introducing them once, you can have them live on a living poster in your classroom or school. I say "living" because you should revisit these principles to see if they make sense for the training you will use them for and if you need to add agreements not previously accounted for.

Sample Community Principles

Here are some sample community principles:

Equity of Voice & Noticing Patterns of Participation   You know the people in your building or class who are vocal and the ones who are not usually vocal when participating. Naming this on the front end will help participants stay metacognitive about who participates in the room. Success is seeing and hearing people who are usually vocal catch themselves if they feel like they are the only ones sharing in a community. When someone catches themselves talking and naming this, it's a perfect queue for the facilitator to invite other voices to share who have not.

Speaking Your Truth (Using "I" statements)   Using "I" statements when speaking about experiences helps avoid dangerous generalizations that lead to stereotyping. Success looks like participants speaking from their own perspectives. Success can also look like people catching themselves when they speak in generalizations.

What's Learned Here Leaves Here, What's Shared Here Stays Here. This principle attempts to ensure consent and confidentiality in what is shared. Oftentimes in racial justice workshops, personal stories are shared among community members to connect to the content. However, we can't control what people do with our stories. To have a little more control over what is shared, we emphasize this principle. Success looks like people not sharing personal stories of others without consent. Success can also look like when personal stories of others are shared without consent, the community keeps each other accountable by naming that and ensuring it doesn't happen again.

Lean into Discomfort Discomfort is where so much of the learning actually happens for people who have not engaged in racial justice work. It is uncomfortable for most people when talking about concepts centering on Asian Americans that intersect with white supremacy, anti-Blackness, colonialism, and more because it is unnatural. Success is when people share that they are learning from the discomfort. An example is when I was a leading DEI facilitator in 2020, and was challenged by a queer-identifying teacher who said that I had not included enough trans and non-binary narratives when teaching introductory lessons on how to support LGBTQIA+ students. This learning was necessary for me to transform how I design curriculum explicitly focused on this intersectional topic.

Calling In & Up vs. Calling Out Calling In & Up means keeping someone accountable in the moment or after a harm has been committed. The "up" portion is facilitating the learning of the individual who committed the harm. I put this first concept in contradiction with "calling out," to lean into possibility and community. Calling out is when someone names something, but there is no learning happening on the perpetrator's side. The facilitator's role is to help conduct that learning or reflection for the perpetrator whether in the moment or at a later time.

Intent vs. Impact (Focusing on Impact) People who have done the harm usually like to focus on their intent and not the harm committed because it's simply easier to deflect. If someone from the marginalized group critiques how you are operating in a space meant to center or empower them, then it's helpful to stop, reflect, listen, and apologize for committing any harm. And then perhaps follow up if the person harmed is willing in that moment or after to dialogue.

Combat Binary Thinking   We touched on this concept in Chapter 5. Combat binary thinking means that we are able to hold multiple perspectives at the same exact time. This leans into the concept of multi-partiality. White dominant logic wants us to be able to name conflict and quickly solve it in a linear way. Most conflict around anti–Asian American sentiment, racism, and violence is more abstract than it is technical. Success acknowledges that we can name white supremacy, while not blaming all white people, and this is mutually understood between white people and people of color. Success acknowledges that we can both be angry at what someone says, but still hold respect for them. It is more realistic to name that we are able to hold multiple truths at once. Success looks like multiple truths being described in any of the given scenarios that follow.

Again, these community principles are not exhaustive. As you build deeper connections with your school community, there will be moments of conflict that require an emphasis on one or more of these principles over others. One important note is to revisit multi-partiality and ensure that Asian American voices are both centered and approached with consent when engaging in the following scenarios.

Framing for Case Study Analysis and Practice

Before launching your staff or students into these case studies, please frame the space with a content warning, signaling that they will be reading moments of anti-Asian hate, violence, and racism similar to how we would frame the anti-Asian hate timeline activity in Chapter 3. Add that if reading these case studies triggers a traumatic response, any participants can do what they need to do to take care of themselves in order to re-engage with the content. For schools that offer this workshop, if you can provide a counselor or psychologist on site to respond to traumatic responses, that is recommended. I realize that this is not always the case for schools.

Directions for Case Study Analysis and Practice (30–45 min)

Here are the steps:

1. Group your participants into groups of three or four.

2. Each group reads through the six scenarios individually.

3. For each scenario, have students read the anti-bias and anti-racist reflection questions (as seen below):

   ◆ How may bias and/or racism be showing up in this scenario?

   ◆ What system(s) of oppression might be reinforced/ perpetuated if we are not careful in how we approach this situation?

   ◆ What are you considering as part of your decision-making process?

   ◆ How would you respond? Why?

   ◆ How is your decision rooted in culturally relevant and sustaining education pillars or beliefs?.

4. Discuss each question.

5. After discussing and workshopping potential ways to under-stand the problem in each case study and ways to respond, invite the groups back into a whole group to discuss each scenario.

6. Capture the overall learnings from the whole group discussion and share this as a resource to your entire school.

Case Studies

The following are six case studies.

SCENARIO 1: LANGUAGE AND RESPONDING TO ANTI-ASIAN STATEMENTS

You teach at a school that serves a student demographic that is 30% Latinx (all-inclusive), 40% African American, 20% Asian American, and 10% white. During a class, one of your students yells out loud "Ching Chong Ching Chong" to an Asian district staff member who walks in the room. Kids start to laugh. You feel like everyone heard this while you're experiencing a formal observation. What do you do?

ANTI-BIAS AND ANTI-RACIST QUESTIONS

- How may bias and/or racism be showing up in this scenario?
- What system(s) of oppression might be reinforced/perpetuated if we are not careful in how we approach this situation?
- What are you considering as part of your decision-making process?
- How would you respond? Why?

SCENARIO 2: ADMINISTRATION

Student A: A football player, identifies as Samoan American and heterosexual.
Student B: A debater, identifies as a Chinese American and is openly non-binary and queer.
The Principal: Black, cisgender man, homosexual, who has been principal for the last seven years.
Scenario: Today is Career Day at Larry Itliong Senior High School. This school is known for sending students who are in the football program on full scholarships to colleges, and some have made it to the NFL. On "Career Day" while you are teaching, Student B gets in a fight with Student A because they were getting bullied in class. When the fight is broken up, you speak with both students that tell their side of the story. Student B reports being called a "F*g" because of wearing makeup and a dress for Career Day. Student A reports that Student B was lying and actually threw something at them from across the room. When you send this report back to admin, by the end of the day you get a message from admin stating that Student B is suspended, while Student A is given detention.

ANTI-BIAS AND ANTI-RACIST QUESTIONS

- How may bias and/or racism be showing up in this scenario?
- What system(s) of oppression might be reinforced/perpetuated if we are not careful in how we approach this situation?
- What are you considering as part of your decision-making process?
- How would you respond? Why?

SCENARIO 3: SCHOOL-PROVIDED CURRICULUM

You're an elementary teacher. Your school provides you with a curriculum to teach from the company Reading A-Z. Your curriculum specialist and principal has stated on numerous occasions how important it is to implement the curriculum with fidelity. As you go through the curriculum, you notice that there are no books that center or include Asian American narratives.

ANTI-BIAS AND ANTI-RACIST QUESTIONS

- How may bias and/or racism be showing up in this scenario?
- What system(s) of oppression might be reinforced/perpetuated if we are not careful in how we approach this situation?
- What are you considering as part of your decision-making process?
- How would you respond? Why?

SCENARIO 4: NAVIGATING YOUR TRIGGERS

During history class you're reading about the history and immigration stories of South Asian Americans and Chinese Americans. You are about to begin where you left off with the previous class and read aloud about the "Coolie Trade." One of your students says, "You can't say that term." Another student replies to you and says, "Oh, are we being the woke police again?"

ANTI-BIAS AND ANTI-RACIST QUESTIONS

- How may bias and/or racism be showing up in this scenario?
- What system(s) of oppression might be reinforced/perpetuated if we are not careful in how we approach this situation?
- What are you considering as part of your decision-making process?
- How would you respond? Why?

SCENARIO 5: A GUEST IN A BLACK AND BROWN SPACE

You are in a meeting at the annual Middle School of Color Conference for your district. This is an opportunity where you get paid to co-design a cross-racial education conference for youth and educators of color. Your school district consists of 10% Asian Americans, 30% Latinx/Latine Americans, 30% African American, and 20% white identifying students. You're talking over the program and notice that there is one Black and one Latinx/Latine identifying keynote speaker throughout the conference. Another team member brings up that we need Asian American representation in keynote speakers. The keynote committee chair says, "We already confirmed these speakers, and plus Asian Americans are really guests in this Black and Brown space."

ANTI-BIAS AND ANTI-RACIST QUESTIONS

- How may bias and/or racism be showing up in this scenario?
- What system(s) of oppression might be reinforced/perpetuated if we are not careful in how we approach this situation?
- What are you considering as part of your decision-making process?
- How would you respond? Why?

SCENARIO 6: RESPONDING TO CRISIS	ANTI-BIAS AND ANTI-RACIST QUESTIONS:
On the news there are two back-to-back mass shootings involving Asian Americans resulting in 20 Asian American deaths and casualties. You are the assistant principal at Lakewood Middle School where the staff and student population identifies as 98% white, 1% Black, and 1% Asian American. You bring this news to your principal expecting that they will hold a moment of silence or create a statement around this tragedy, but instead your principal just says, "Damn, I saw that." They then transition to another topic.	• How may bias and/or racism be showing up in this scenario? • What system(s) of oppression might be reinforced/perpetuated if we are not careful in how we approach this situation? • What are you considering as part of your decision-making process? • How would you respond? Why?

A Movement, Not a Moment

You just learned about different moments of anti-Asian hate, violence, and racism that may manifest in any given school. All of these scenarios are based on personal experiences having been a student, an educator, and instructional coach in schools. Remember the work to be pro–Asian American is somatic. Practicing how to identify bias and racism in the Asian American community is step one to allyship, and taking action is the next! The following are more resources to continue your learning.

TITLE/LINK	AUTHOR(S)	WHAT'S IN THIS RESOURCE?
Appendix B: Role Playing www.learningforjustice.org/ magazine/publications/speak- up-at-school/appendices/appendix- b-roleplaying	Learning for Justice	This resource offers a variety of anti-bias and anti-racist role playing scenarios for educators.
Five Ways that Educators can Combat Anti-Asian Sentiment hechingerreport.org/teacher- voice-coronavirus-doesnt- discriminate/	Tony DelaRosa in the Hechinger Report	This resource offers immediate ways to address anti-Asian sentiment in and outside of the classroom. It puts an emphasis on normalizing pro–Asian American narratives in schools.

(Continues)

(Continued)

TITLE/LINK	AUTHOR(S)	WHAT'S IN THIS RESOURCE?
Facilitators Guide for Departmental Discussions on Race blogs.umsl.edu/diversity/ files/2020/06/Facilitator-Guide-for-Departmental-Discussions-about-Race-UMSL-1-1.pdf	Marlo Goldstein Hode at the University of Missouri	This resource offers broad strategies on how to facilitate discussions on race with staff members. There is a focus on what to do to prepare for the discussion and what to do during the discussion.

Chapter 15

Asian America and Abolition

LEARNING OBJECTIVES:

◆ Practitioners will understand the concept of abolition (knowledge).

◆ Practitioners will shift their understanding from allyship to kinship (mindset).

◆ Practitioners will learn school practices that embody abolition that aligns with a pro–Asian American lens (skill).

The Personal Is Political

Will they dance a revolution or will they wallflower reform?

I bring us back to this line in my poem because it is a north star toward action. When I say, "dance a revolution," it is an emphasis on choosing revolutions over reforms. To embody a pro–Asian American lens in schools, we must shift from reformist mindsets, policies, and ways of being to abolition.

An example of a reformist policy is what we saw in March 2020. When anti-Asian hate reports skyrocketed beginning in March 2020, many celebrities and political leaders rose to the occasion to demand reforms, which included more police presence. I get it. We live in a society where we are conditioned to think that the police are the only thing that keeps us safe. But that's not true for everyone. Through a study by economist Morgan Williams at New York University, more police presence in a city has many effects. On one hand, Williams suggests that more police presence can lead to fewer homicides for some cities, which is a data point that people like to apply to every city and context because of convenience. In cities that are more densely populated by Black people, policing can lead to more racial profiling and arrests toward the Black community.

When thinking of combating anti-Asian hate, violence, and racism we have to do so in collective liberation, an antidote to white supremacy culture. White supremacy culture feeds on individualism, paternalism, and a false sense of urgency. The demand for more policing is rooted in individualism because it renders the issues of anti-Asian hate to an interpersonal conflict, when we know (up to this point in the book) anti-Asian hate is born out of white supremacy, which requires a collective approach. The demands are paternalistic because they rely on paternal labor markets in the form of policing to solve deeply entrenched issues. Lastly, demanding more police presence leads to a false sense of urgency around the type of solutions that we are willing to design and create. So, of course, celebrities and political leaders called for more policing.

When we think about anti-Asian hate, violence, and racism in and out of schools, I want you to pair this book with the work of abolitionist teaching. But what is abolitionist teaching? Dr. Bettina Love, author of *We Want to Do More Than Survive*, says in an interview with ACSD (Association for Supervision and Curriculum Development) that "Abolitionist teaching looks different in every school...It comes from a critical race lens and applies methods like protest, boycotting, and calling out other teachers who are racist, homophobic, or Islamophobic." Dr. Bettina Love founded the Abolitionist Teaching Network to provide educators ways to embody an abolitionist lens to education. Dr. Love calls the current education system an "educational survival complex," one that is "built on the suffering of students of color in which they are never educated to thrive, only to survive."

She describes abolitionist teaching as both a practice and way of life, which is similar to ethnic studies. When thinking of taking a pro–Asian American lens to your school, Asian American liberation requires that you root this lens in the abolitionist approach. Remember being pro–Asian American is contingent on combating anti-Blackness and embodying a pro-Black way of being. When thinking of embodying a pro–Asian American lens in schools, you are taking an intersectional, cross-racial, and anti-colonial way of being. You are not using the master's tools to "dismantle the master's house" (Audre Lorde) — you are imaginative, radical, bold, determined, and urgent.

In the "Praxis: Action and Reflection" section, you will learn a few principles that will help you root your pro–Asian American lens in abolitionist education practices. I'm only including a few because I recommend reading the entirety of *We Want to Do More Than Survive* to gain greater nuance on what this means for you and your school. *Teaching the Invisible Race: Embodying a Pro–Asian American Lens in Schools* is full of abolitionist teaching practices and ways of thinking and being. You will also be challenged to reconnect to previous chapters and reflect on how they embody an abolitionist education practice.

Praxis: Action and Reflection

The following are a list of six abolitionist teaching principles from *We Want to Do More Than Survive*. I have contextualized them to intersect Asian American experiences in schools. After each description of the principle, there is a reflection question, which is geared toward education practitioners. In terms of examples, you'll hear from my own and a few other Asian American Avengers that I bring back to share their experiences. I delineate who's speaking by adding our names at the end of the description.

Abolitionist Teaching Principles and Reflection Questions

Refusing to take part in zero-tolerance policies and the school to prison pipeline
Zero-tolerance policies leads to the school to prison pipeline. This is the same concept I referred to with regard to police arresting people for petty crimes. Instead of police, within the school system, teachers who use zero-tolerance punish students

for petty offenses or for being resistant to work. As an administrator you refuse this type of policy by creating policies that require teachers to leverage their relationships to redirect students or seek clarity when students are resistant to work.

REFLECTION QUESTIONS

When you think about a pro–Asian American lens and zero-tolerance policies, what comes to mind? Why?

Opposing English-only education   For Asian American students who come in with dual language experience, weaving in the home language can help foster inclusion, belonging, and lead to Asian American students being active in class. The following is an example where not being inclusive of home language negatively impacts Asian American students:

> "The most marginalized Hmong students at UHS were long-term English learners who experienced multiple forms of vulnerability, including poverty. These students suffered from lack of belonging...Their status as long-term English learners marked them as academically challenged and as problematic exceptions to the stereotype of Asian Americans as high-achieving model minorities...[they] were rendered hypervisible as failed model minorities..."

> (Lee et al., 2022)

> "I remember one day in Kindergarten I tried explaining that I had a doctor's appointment to take an X-ray. I did not know the word for "X-ray" in English, and only knew it in Shanghainese, the dialect spoken in Shanghai, China. Although there were a few Chinese-speaking classmates in my space, no one spoke Shanghainese and knew what I was talking about. This is one of multiple moments where I felt misunderstood. Throughout my own schooling, I can recall English-only education, and the only times where my dialect was asked about felt like an exoticization of my linguistic knowledge."

> —Alice Tsui

This excerpt comes from Dr. Stacey Lee's recent research in *Resisting Asian American Invisibility: The Politics of Race and Education*, which focused on the Hmong population. This research is a powerful tool in understanding how neoliberal education policies impact Hmong youth at a systems level.

REFLECTION QUESTIONS

When you think about a pro–Asian American lens and English-only education, what comes to mind? Why?

Acknowledging and accepting that American schools exist in a racist system. Asian Americans are a part of a racist history of exclusion. We see this through exclusion in curriculum and literacy tests. We saw this in the anti-Asian hate timeline in Chapter 3. Acknowledging that the United States education system was and still is not designed for Asian Americans to combat the model minority myth and the perpetual foreigner stereotype, helps you reframe how you design your classroom from the class policies, procedures, culture, and more.

"The first time I heard this framing was in a training by Spring Up, an organization that focuses on transformative justice and consent education. The facilitators Stas and Leander framed our training with the notion that schools are racist systems because they are designed to advantage some over others, which require education actors to take an active anti-racist and abolitionist lens into our work as educators to change outcomes for systematically and intentionally underserved communities."

—*Tony DelaRosa*

REFLECTION QUESTIONS

When you think about a pro–Asian American lens and acknowledging that the United States education system is racist, what comes to mind? Why?

Accountability of harm   Often when harm is committed toward Asian Americans in schools, the expectation is for us not to confront the perpetrator. This is part of the model minority myth, which instills that we are "good immigrants" and won't act aggressively during conflict. It also reinforces that we won't respond to the harm at all, rendering us stereotypically "weak."

This translates in the classroom in ways where teachers don't respond appropriately or at all to moments of anti-Asian sentiment. It's two-pronged, because statements like "ching chong" are not seen as racist, teachers ignore the response, or teachers say at most "that's not funny" and leave the accountability to that extent. The teacher should address that statements like this are racist if this happened in a whole group and follow through with a repair conversation. In abolitionist teaching practices, it is up to the student harmed to create the terms of accepting repair from the perpetrator.

REFLECTION QUESTIONS

When you think about a pro–Asian American lens and accountability from harm, what comes to mind? Why?

Homeplace

"This concept of "homeplace" is taken from bell hooks. It describes the type of culture that feels like "home." Dr. Bettina Love describes in her book, "'homeplace' is a space where Black folks truly matter to each other, where souls are nurtured, comforted, and fed. Homeplace is a community, typically led by women, where White power and the damages done by it are healed by loving Blackness and restoring dignity" (Love, 83)." While being Pro-Asian American acknowledges the injustices, the destination for our work is Asian American joy and possibility. We encourage this through art, love, and healing"

—Kabby Hong (2022 WI Teacher of the Year)

"When I think of a homeplace for Asian Americans, I think about the club that I advise which is The Asian Student Association (TASA) at Verona Area High School. It's made up almost entirely of Asian American high school students, and for many of my kids it's the only place where they are the majority. They can walk in and see people that look like them and have similar experiences. There is a short-hand that all of us can understand. The growth and popularity of TASA is directly connected to how it feeds and nurtures the soul of my kids. Instead of feeling invisible, my kids can finally be seen. Instead of staying small, my kids can be big/bold with who they are. TASA might be the only place in my students' lives where their Asian American identity is fully embraced and visible. Home is where you can release the armor you wear on a daily basis and be yourself - be vulnerable. I see our TASA club meetings as a second home for many of my students."

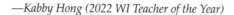

—Kabby Hong (2022 WI Teacher of the Year)

Another example of homeplace is Chundou Alex Her's artivist space co-created with their Hmong American students. Chundou is a colleague at UW-Madison in the Curriculum and Instruction PhD program. Hearing how Chundou encourages and creates intentional spaces for their youth to create radical art that reveals and conceals aspects of their own personal and collective Hmong American stories is so powerful.

REFLECTION QUESTIONS

When you think about a pro–Asian American lens and homeplace, what comes to mind? Why?

Freedom dreaming "Freedom dreaming is imagining worlds that are just, representing people's full humanity, centering people left on the edges, thriving in solidarity with folx from different identities who have struggled together for justice, and knowing that dreams are just around the corner with the might of people power" (Love, 103). For this book, I've demonstrated how Asian Americans have leveraged freedom dreaming through learning from the Black Power Movement and hip-hop. Robin D. G. Kelley, author of *Freedom Dreams: The Black Radical Imagination*, concedes that racist anti-Black power may never be fully overthrown. If that is the case, then we can concede the same thing about anti-Asian hate and racism. Kelley says that subverting Black racist systems requires "divining Black futures," therefore inspiring the next generation of Black freedom fighters (Warren, 4).

So with regard to schools, building the radical imagination of every student to imagine Asian Americans in the future and Asian Americans that embody multitudes is a form of freedom dreaming toward Asian Americans. Another way that focuses on building the freedom dreaming habits of Asian American youth and teachers is to celebrate Asian American freedom fighters all throughout the year.

REFLECTION QUESTIONS

When you think about a pro–Asian American lens and freedom dreaming, what comes to mind?

A Movement, Not a Moment

Ending this book on abolitionist teaching practices that include Asian Americans is a radical act in and of itself because we rarely get to see the terms "abolition" and "Asian American" in the same sentence. That is done on purpose through the model minority myth. White supremacy culture does not want Asian Americans or allies of Asian Americans to join the fight for collective liberation, because it survives off the partition of people of color and marginalized communities. The following are more resources to learn about Asians Americans and abolition:

Title/Link	Author(s)	What's in This Resource?
Abolitionist Teaching Network Guide abolitionistteaching network.org/ guide	The Abolitionist Teaching Network	This resource gives teaching mindsets, habits, and practices on how to embody abolitionist teaching in the classroom.
Abolitionist Teaching and Learning with Bettina Love snfpaideia.upenn.edu/ abolitionist-teaching-and-learning-with-bettina-l-love/	Sarah Ropp in University of Pennsylvania Paideia Program	This resource gives both an objective and personal summary of Dr. Bettina Love's book *We Want to Do More Than Survive.*
Asian Americans for Abolition: Finding our place in a movement www.mochimag.com/ activism/asian-americans-for-abolition/	Abigail Lee in *Mochi Magazine*	This resource dives into what the surveillance state means, the attack on bodily autonomy, and how Asians can get involved in the movement for abolition.
Envisioning Abolition Democracy harvardlawreview.org/ 2019/04/envisioning-abolition-democracy/	Allegra M. McLeod in *The Harvard Law Review*	This resource defines abolition democracy and gives case studies where abolition democracy works in practice.
Anti-Asian violence is a serious issue, but more policing isn't the solution: Why do business groups keep speaking for Asian America? www.washingtonpost.com/ outlook/2022/03/16/anti-asian-violence-is-serious-problem-policing-isnt-solution/	Crystal Jing Luo in *The Washington Post*	This resource outlines the connections between business owners, gentrification, the model minority myth, and tensions between the Black and Asian community in Oakland.

Epilogue

The Game Board: Filipino
Coach Edition

after Lauren Lisa Ng "The Game Board"
Here's how you play:
You wake up in a house so move ahead three spaces
because you've "made it."
You head to work, mask up, and drive to a school in North
Miami to observe one of your elementary school teachers.
They are holding a restorative justice circle, just like
you taught,
so move forward one space.
You notice a few students stare at you and
automatically ask you:
Are you Chinese? Did you bring Corona here?
Triggered, move back a step.
One student whispers across the room and another
virus spreads,
a wildfire throughout the classroom.
Move back two places again.
You muster the strength to pull this student aside
and remind him that this is not so different than what his
ancestors dealt with
what he may deal with, and what he just added to . . . you
invite an apology
he nods in agreement, apologizes, and we move forward
two steps.
I transition to South Miami to observe another
but the game board is still Black and white.
You head into a high school math classroom and they are
doing a gallery walk.
It looks super engaged, so go ahead and move forward
three steps.
Then kids notice you, one waves

and another yells "Ching Chong Ching Chong" in
their group.
Pause and scan. . . I can't make out who, so step back again.
The teacher heard too but didn't react, so step back again.
Another kid yells hey Squid Game! I need some help.
So move back further two steps
You remember you've played this hand before, so stay idle.
Just smile and breathe, remember your somatics
The words of your coach
a healed person can heal people
Then move forward and try to focus on the lesson.
But what actually is the lesson here?
Is it coaching the teacher to teach their students to master this
formula on paper?
y = mx + b, a slope to meritocracy?
or are we trying to intercept something else?
Is it intercepting issues for the teacher?
What even is a teachable moment
If we are not prepared for the teachable movement?
There is no cheat code. No moves to safety.
The unlearning is a slow, hard, and wise hand,
Illegible at the moment, but nonetheless true.

I wrote this poem right after one of my observations during Asian Pacific Islander Heritage Month while coaching teachers in Miami-Dade in 2021. This poem was a snapshot of what some Asian Americans have to deal with when schools are not pro–Asian American.

Getting bullied as an adult by kids during a lesson where your role is to be a fly on the wall is such a gaslighting feeling. The adult side says, "Yo it's just a kid, shrug it off." But the Asian side says, "Nah, this is a teaching moment." Then the coach says, "Well if I intervene, then I just took a teaching moment away from the teacher who saw the situation unfold." I don't blame the students for not knowing better. Nor do I blame the teachers for not responding at the moment, because the teacher was receptive to feedback. I do blame the system that doesn't support the teachers' development in embodying a pro–Asian American lens.

I do blame an institution that sees Asian Americans and any other ethnoracial group as an afterthought or as disposable.

Knowing that I could go from one school in North Miami that is predominantly African American to another school in South Miami that is predominantly Central American and broadly Latiné identifying and experience the same type of anti-Asian sentiment was both frustrating and enlightening. I knew there were more instances like these in and out of education, and I knew I wanted to be a part of the solution, which is why I wrote this book and why my research is focused on Asian American ethnic studies policy and critical race theory. If I don't do something, then one day my son (and others) will eventually encounter the same anti-Asian hate.

The bullying I dealt with as a student and adult is nothing compared to what we've witnessed over the last few years since the inception of the pandemic. We know that crimes have been reported in the thousands across the country, but simply stating this statistic is not enough. In a pro–Asian American lens, if we have the consent of the victim attacked or the family of the victim, we have to name the victims and know who they were before their attacks. They are or were everyday people like you and me, trying to live their lives in peace, trying to define their American dreams.

I'm going to name a few with their location, and I encourage you to learn about their stories: Vicha Ratanapakdee who was tackled to death in San Francisco, the six Chinese and Korean women murdered in Atlanta (not naming their names due to lack of family consent), Nirmal Singh who was punched in Queens, Vilma Kari who was stomped on in Manhattan, Woom Sing Tse who was shot in Chicago, Tyler who was attacked at the University of Cincinnati, the Asian American family who was stabbed at a Sam's Club in Texas, and countless more.

Fast-forward to Lunar New Year in 2023, a date that ushers in hope, prosperity, joy, and community across the Asian diaspora. I posted on social media the image shown in Figure E.1 on January 22, 2023.

The next day on January 23rd, I'm greeted with the headline "10 dead, 10 wounded in mass shooting in Monterey Park, California, with suspect found dead" from ABC News. Not even 48 hours later we hear about more Asian Americans dead by a murder spree in

FIGURE E.1 A tweet that says "Happiest #LunarNewYear2023 to my Asian diaspora who celebrate on Jan 22nd ushering in hope, community, and prosperity (Chinese, Vietnamese, Korean, Malaysian, Tibetan, Indonesian, Filipino, & more). Here are 6 learnings a/b #LunarNewYear in the Philippines #yearoftherabbit2023"

Half Moon Bay, California. My first thought was — how will schools at all levels talk about these events? Will they even mention them, cast the American flag at half-mast, or echo the names of the dead? Again, *how will they hold us?*

That last question was the title of one of my poems and the question that drove this book. How will education practitioners hold us? My solution was breaking down what it means to take on a pro–Asian American lens, a perspective that is active. With Asian American K–12 education policy sweeping the country because of coalitions such as Asian Americans Advancing Justice and Make Us Visible, I have hope for change. As shown in Figure E.2, "education" was one of the top two recommended responses from the community to combat anti-Asian hate, violence, and racism according to the 2022 Stop AAPI Hate Report Card.

Educating people is why I wrote this book with a critical lens. I'm doing my part in a movement of many. My ancestors opened the door for this book. *Teaching The Invisible Race: Embodying a Pro–Asian American Lens in Schools* is an intervention. With schools not resourced enough to translate ethnic studies policy into practice with nuance and care, I know we have a long way to go.

Let this book be a pathway. Let this book be a clarion call to education practitioners saying that we mustn't wait for education

FIGURE E.2 2022 Stop AAPI Hate Report Card

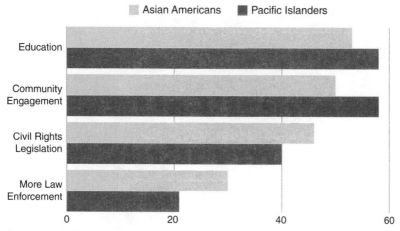

Most Effective Solutions in Addressing Anti-AAPI Hate (Nationally)

Asian Americans ■ Pacific Islanders

Source: The 2022 Stop AAPI Hate Report Card

policy to save us, because it won't. During AAPI Heritage Month this year, Florida passed an Asian American education policy but in isolation while AP Black History was rejected, LGBTQIA+ identities are being attacked, and social justice spending is being cut. The AAPI Coalition of Wisconsin just got a public hearing for Asian American education, and if it passes, it will take some time to translate policy into practice. Education policy is technically the easy part according to Dr. Jason Oliver Chang (University of Connecticut). The journey to teaching Asian American history out of invisibility and omission starts with you and ends in collective liberation.

Glossary

Abolition   the mindset, belief, or action of abolishing a practice, system, or institution.

Abolitionist teaching   a way of teaching and life that embodies abolitionist practices such as creating homeplace, rejecting English-only education, freedom dreaming, and more (Love, 2019).

Acculturation   when a non-dominant group takes on the mindsets, beliefs, and actions that mirror that of the dominant group but maintain aspects of their own unique culture and value systems.

Affinity group   a group formed of shared interests, identities, and/or goals where particular identities belong.

Allyship   the concept of becoming an ally to a group or movement.

Anti-Black racism   racism that targets the Black community.

Asian American Avengers   a term used to describe any Asian American person fighting for the collective liberation of Asians and Asian American people in the United Studies.

Asian Crit   also known as Asian Critical Race Theory, Asian Crit is the focus of applying CRT to the lives of Asians and Asian Americans.

Asian settler colonialism   when Asians settle in a territory and reinstate colonialist practices and policies on that land and its native or indigenous people.

Assimilation   when a non-dominant group takes on mindsets, beliefs, and actions that mirror that of the dominant group in order to survive.

Baklâ   means third gender or queer in the Philippines.

Baybaylans   precolonial Philippine shamans and chieftains who had/have the ability to communicate with the spirit world, and often identify as woman, femme, trans, or non-binary.

Black-white binary   also known as the Black-white paradigm, is a presentation of racial history that only focuses on a linear story between white and Black Americans.

Coolie   a dated and offensive term to describe unskilled labor from India, China, and other Asian countries.

Cisgender   when your gender identity matches your sex assignment at birth.

Code-switching   the act of switching cultural ways of being or languages depending on different settings.

Collective liberation   the concept of liberation tied to multiple people and groups as opposed to liberation being achieved through individual means.

Colonization   a concept where another country or dominant group exerts complete control over another country or group.

Colonial mentality   the residual effect of colonization that influences the psyche to embrace aspects of the dominant group doing the colonizing.

Community-engaged scholarship   Community-engaged scholarship (CES) involves the researcher in a mutually beneficial relationship or partnership with the community and results in scholarship deriving from teaching, discovery, integration, application, or engagement.

Counter-storytelling   a method of telling the stories of those people whose experiences are not often told (Solorzano & Yosso, 2002).

Crip ecologies   describe the messy, diverse, and profoundly beautiful ecosystems which exist for disabled people (Ortiz, 2022).

Critical consciousness   coined by Paulo Freire as having a critical understanding of self in relation to the world that exposes social and political contradictions.

Critical race praxis   a concept of bridging concepts of critical race theory to the iterative cycle of practice and reflection (Yamamoto, 1997).

Critical race theory   a legal and academic theory born from the 1970s that acknowledges that racism is more than the result of individual bias and prejudice. It is embedded in laws, policies, and institutions that uphold and reproduce racial inequalities.

Culturally relevant and sustaining education   education that ensures equity for all students and seeks to eliminate systemic institutional racial and cultural barriers that inhibit the success of all students — particularly those who have been intentionally and historically underrepresented.

Data disaggregation   separation of compiled information into smaller units to elucidate underlying trends and patterns.

Diaspora   a diffusion of people from their homeland across many places.

Diasporic longing   a longing for one's ethnoracial homeland.

Decolonization   the act of identifying the impacts of colonization, freeing oneself from the impacts of colonization.

Enculturation   when one reinforces values and systems of belief and practice of the culture they are already situated in.

Ekphrasis   a literary device in helping describe artwork.

Equity   this concept recognizes that each person or group has different circumstances, experiences, and needs; therefore when resources are allocated, the precise type and amount of resources and opportunities are given. This is often compared to equality, which refers to everyone getting the same type and same amount of a resource.

Erasure   the concept of a group and history being erased or omitted from something; for this book, it's the erasure of Asian Americans from United States education.

Ethnoracial matching   when matching teachers with students that share a similar ethnoracial background.

Exploitation   the act of treating someone unfairly and benefiting off of their labor.

Fetishization making someone the object of sexual desire based on an aspect of their identity.

Freedom dreaming a way of being that visualizes a future of joy and collective liberation, where those who are marginalized are leading and celebrated (Robin D.G. Kelley).

Gaslighting a process of psychological manipulation where the abuser attempts to put doubt or confusion in their victim's mind; a typical example of this is denying someone else's lived experience.

Gender the social, psychological, cultural, and behavioral aspects of being a man, woman, or other gender identity.

Gender fluid denoting or relating to a person who does not identify as having a single unchanging gender.

Heteronormativity a world view that promotes heterosexuality as the norm or preferred sexual orientation.

Homeplace a hooksian concept describing the type of culture that feels like "home;" applying Dr. Bettina Love's description of homeplace, which contextualizes this for Black people, for this book it can mean a space where Asian Americans truly matter to each other, where souls are nurtured, comforted, and fed.

Homogenize to make a diverse group into a monolithic group that resembles sameness.

Imperialism a policy of extending a country's power through diplomacy or coercion.

Interracial praxis the concept of cross-racial interactive practice of action and reflection.

Intersectionality the concept of when multiple identities intersect; other scholars use the term "enmeshed" identities to emphasize the fusion and inability to separate multiple identities after they intersect.

Isang Bagsak educational framework the Tagalog term "Isang Bagsak" connotes the concept of collective liberation; the educational framework expands this concept into tangible ways collective liberation can manifest in any given space.

Kapwa   a Filipino core value that signifies "interconnectedness" between people.

Kinship   a combination of understanding of the land we inhabit, centering the wisdom of youth and women, centering ceremony and relationship to our ancestors, fostering relational accountability, and centering culture as medicine and holistic healing as opposed to additive matter (Jolivette, 2021).

Model minority myth   a concept that sees Asian Americans and other immigrants as good and ideal minorities seen from a white dominant gaze.

Minoritized   to make a person or group subordinate to the dominant group.

Multi-partiality   the ability to hold multiple truths while advantaging the most disadvantaged identities in a given space.

Ontology   a way of operating or being.

Orientalism   a way of seeing and defining Asian cultures as inferior, backward, exotic, or in need of rescuing by the western world.

Perpetual foreigner stereotype   the concept that Asian Americans are always seen and treated as foreigners or outsiders of the dominant group.

Plurality   psychological phenomenon in which a body can feature multiple distinct or overlapping consciousnesses, each with its own degree of individuality.

Praxis   the iterative practice of action and reflection coined by Paolo Freire.

Racial capitalism   a system of capitalism that uses race or racial labor as the unit of value exchange.

Racism   an interpersonal or systemic act that oppresses a particular person or group based on their racial identity.

Reclaiming   taking something for the means of self-liberation.

Racialization   a sociological concept and political process of ascribing ethnic or racial identities to a relationship, social practice, or group that did not identify itself as such for the purpose of domination and social exclusion.

Settler colonialism   a system of oppression based on genocide and colonialism, that aims to displace a population of a nation (oftentimes indigenous people) and replace it with a new settler population.

Sexual orientation   a person's identity in relation to the gender or genders to which they are sexually attracted.

Somatic   a term that characterizes the body as separate from the mind.

Stories   interpretations of what happens to people, places, and events (Aguilar, 2013).

Tiger parent   a trope that paints Asian parents as extremely aggressive and sometimes oppressive when raising their child.

Undocu-Asian   being an undocumented Asian or Asian American.

Undocumented   not having the "legal" documentation. This is used in place of "illegal," which is a social construct and carries negative perceptions of a person.

White gaze   a lens in which advantages a perspective stemming from white dominant culture and protects white comfort.

White saviorism   a trope of white actors saving historically marginalized people from plight by providing resources or direct action.

White supremacy   a belief system that white people and whiteness constitutes a superior race and should therefore dominate society, typically to the exclusion or detriment of other racial and ethnic groups.

Yellowface   the act of a non-Asian person dressing and playing the part of an Asian or Asian American person, which is different from cultural appreciation of someone dressing up as a specific Asian character because they admire them; yellowface usually comes with the non-Asian person benefiting from dressing up as an Asian person without bearing the consequences of being Asian or Asian American in a racialized world.

Yellow peril/Asian menace   an offensive term where Asian Americans are seen as "menaces" to society; this term originated in the late 19th century.

References

Aikau, H. K., & Gonzalez, V. V. (Eds.). (2019). *Detours: A Decolonial Guide to Hawaii*. Duke University Press, 1–45.

Asante-Muhammad, D., & Sim, S. (2020, May 14). Racial wealth snapshot: Asian Americans and the Racial Wealth Divide. National Community Reinvestment Coalition. https://ncrc.org/racial-wealth-snapshot-asian-americans-and-the-racial-wealth-divide/#_ftn8

Barrett, K. U. (2022, January 3). To hold the grief & the growth[1]: On crip ecologies. Poetry Foundation. https://www.poetryfoundation.org/poetrymagazine/articles/156938/to-hold-the-grief-the-growth1-on-crip-ecologies

Blouin, B. (2022, May 12). 5 Asian-American war heroes we should've learned about in school. Veteran Life. https://veteranlife.com/military-history/asian-american-war-heroes/

Boggs, G. L. (2011). The next American revolution: Sustainable activism for the twenty-first century.

Bolen, D. (Ed.) (2017). . (Vols. 1–4). SAGE Publications, Inc. https://doi.org/10.4135/9781483381411

Buenavista, T. L. (2018). Model (undocumented) minorities and "illegal" immigrants: Centering Asian Americans and US carcerality in undocumented student discourse. *Race, Ethnicity and Education*, 21(1), 78–91.

Buenavista, T. L., & Chen, A. C. (2013). Intersections and crossroads: A counter-story of an undocumented Pinay college student.

Cheung, A. (2021, August 21). Colonialism: Its impact on the Asian American Experience. Cold Tea Collective. https://coldteacollective.com/colonialism-asian-american-experience/

Chin, F., & Chan, J. P. (1972). Racist Love. Dartmouth.edu. https://www.dartmouth.edu/~hist32/Hist33/chin%20Racist%20Love.pdf

Cho, E. Y. (2019). *Invisible illegality: The double bind of being Asian and undocumented* [Doctoral dissertation, University of California, Berkeley]. ProQuest Dissertations Publishing. https://escholarship.org/uc/item/0nk070sx.

Choy, C. C. (2015). A Different Mirror: Philippine International Adoption through the Lens of Brillante Mendoza's Foster Child. *Verge: Studies in Global Asias*, 1(1), 212–229. https://doi.org/10.5749/vergstudglobasia.1.1.0212

Colucci, E. (2019, May 8). This art exhibition transforms Lesbian Archives into a powerful ode to queer history. Them. https://www.them.us/story/shame-is-the-first-betrayer

Cooc, N. (2019). Disparities in the Enrollment and Timing of Special Education for Asian American and Pacific Islander Students. *The Journal of Special Education*, 53(3), 177–190. https://doi.org/10.1177/0022466919839029

Curammeng, E., Buenavista, T. L., & Cariaga, S. (2017). Asian American Critical Race Theory: Origins, Directions, and Praxis. Center for Critical Race Studies UCLA, (9), 1–4. https://issuu.com/almaiflores/docs/ec_tlb_sc_asianam_crt

DelaRosa, T. (2021, October 26). Educators Making a Difference: Building Affinity Space for Asian American Teachers. Retrieved May 12, 2023, from https://smithsonianapa.org/learn/learn-archives/affinity-spaces/.

De Leon, A. (2021, October 19). Firsting Filipinos: The 1587 Morro Bay Landing and Asian America's Settler Colonial Historiography. Sulo The Philippine Studies Initiative at NYU. https://wp.nyu.edu/spsi/the-global-philippine-studies-forum/events/previous-events/firsting-filipinos/

Dizikes, P. (2013, January 7). The hidden history of bengali harlem. The hidden history of Bengali Harlem. Retrieved April 26, 2023, from https://news.mit.edu/2013/vivek-bald-hidden-history-of-bengali-harlem-0107

Dunn, D. S., & Andrews, E. E. (2015). Person-first and identity-first language: Developing psychologists' cultural competence using disability language. *American Psychologist*, 70(3), 255–264. https://doi.org/10.1037/a0038636

Editor, N. B. (2021, May 5). Recognizing Asian and Pacific Islander Educators with the National Teacher and Principal Survey (NTPS). nces.ed.gov. https://nces.ed.gov/blogs/nces/post/recognizing-asian-and-pacific-islander-educators-with-the-national-teacher-and-principal-survey-ntps

Enriquez, L. E. (2019). Border-hopping Mexicans, law-abiding Asians, and racialized illegality: Analyzing undocumented college students' experiences through a relational lens.

Equal Justice Initiative. (n.d.). Jan. 19, 1930: White mobs attack Filipino farmworkers in Watsonville, California. calendar.eji.org. https://calendar.eji.org/racial-injustice/jan/19

Fadiman, A. (2012). *The Spirit Catches You and You Fall Down: A Hmong Child, Her American Doctors, and the Collision of Two Cultures*. Macmillan.

Feldblum, M., Hubbard, S., Lim, A., Penichet-Paul, C., & Siegel, H. (2021). Undocumented students in higher education: How many students are in U.S. colleges and universities, and who are they? The Presidents' Alliance on Higher Education and Immigration.

Fields-Cruz, L. (2021, September 28). Trauma Porn: A Media Obsession Worth Eradicating: What can Black storytellers do about it? Black Public Media. https://blackpublicmedia.org/eradicating-americas-obsession-with-trauma-porn/

FilVetREP. (n.d.). The Filipino Veterans Recognition and education project. FilVetREP. Retrieved May 12, 2023, from https://filvetrep.org/

Fresco, C. (n.d.). Cannery Workers' and Farm Laborers' Union 1933-39: Their Strength in Unity. Cannery Workers' and farm laborers' union 1933-39: Their strength in Unity - Seattle Civil Rights and labor history project. https://depts.washington.edu/civilr/cwflu.htm

Ghandi, L. (2021, May 3). The Asian American women who fought to make their mark in WWII. History.com. https://www.history.com/news/asian-american-women-wwii-contributions

Gonyea, D. (2022, February 20). There's been an alarming spike in violence against women of Asian descent in the U.S. NPR. https://www.npr.org/2022/02/20/1082012448/theres-been-an-alarming-spike-in-violence-against-women-of-asian-descent-in-the-us.

Gutierrez, R. A. R. E. (2022). *Racialized realities at the intersection of race and undocumented status: A critical narrative inquiry into the lives of undocumented Asian students in higher education* [Doctoral dissertation, University of California, Los Angeles]. ProQuest Dissertations Publishing. https://escholarship.org/uc/item/0307x0ff.

Harry, B., & Klingner, J. (2022). *Why Are So Many Students of Color in Special Education?: Understanding Race and Disability in Schools*. Teachers College Press.

Ho, S. (2020). Canfei to canji: The freedom of being loud. In Wong, A. (Ed.) *Disability visibility: First-person stories from the twenty-first century* (pp. 112–135). Knopf Doubleday Publishing Group.

Hourihan K.L., Fraundorf S.H., Benjamin A.S. Same faces, different labels: generating the cross-race effect in face memory with social category information. *Mem Cognit.* 2013 Oct;41(7):1021–31. doi: 10.3758/ s13421-013-0316-7. PMID: 23546969; PMCID: PMC3740049.

Huang, C. (2021). Representation, Redistribution and Revolution: A Conversation with Viet Thanh Nguyen. *Asian American Policy Review*, 32. https://aapr.hkspublications.org/2022/05/27/ representation-redistribution-and-revolution-a-conversation-with-viet-thanh-nguyen/

Iftikar, S.J. & Museus, S.D. (2018). On the utility of Asian critical (AsianCrit) theory in the field of education, *International Journal of Qualitative Studies in Education*, 31:10, 935–949, DOI: 10.1080/09518398.2018.1522008

Institute for Education Sciences. (n.d.). The NCES Fast Facts on Teacher characteristics and trends. National Center for Education Statistics (NCES). https://nces.ed.gov/fastfacts/ display.asp?id=28

Is an Interpreter Needed at the IEP Meeting?2016, September). Center for Parent Information and Resources. https://www. parentcenterhub.org/interpreter/

Ishizuka, K. and Stephens, R. (2019). The Cat is Out of the Bag: Orientalism, Anti-Blackness, and White Supremacy in Dr. Seuss's Children's Books. *Research on Diversity in Youth Literature*, Vol. 1: Iss. 2, Article 4.

Kameya, H. (2012, November 30). IN MEMORY OF TAKENORI "TAK" YAMAMOTO: PIONEER JAPANESE AMERICAN GAY ACTIVIST[weblog]. Retrieved May 11, 2023, from https:// sfvjacl.weebly.com/news/in-memory-of-takenori-tak-yama moto-pioneer-japanese-american-gay-activist.

Kim, C. J. (1999). The Racial Triangulation of Asian Americans. *Politics & Society*, 27(1), 105–138. https://doi.org/10.1177/ 0032329299027001005

Kim, S. M., & Yellow Horse, A. J. (2018). Undocumented Asians. *Contexts*, 17(4), 70–71.

Kochhar, R., & Cilluffo, A. (2018, August 12). Income inequality in the U.S. is rising most rapidly among Asians. Pew Research Center's Social & Demographic Trends Project. https://www.pew research.org/social-trends/2018/07/12/income-inequality-in-the-u-s-is-rising-most-rapidly-among-asians/

Kuppers, P. (2022, January 3). Crip Ecologies: Changing Orientation. Poetry Foundation. https://www.poetry foundation.org/poetrymagazine/articles/156939/crip-ecologies-changing-orientation

Ladson-Billings, G. (2009). The Dreamkeepers: Successful teachers of African American children.

Lawrence-Lightfoot, S. (2016). Commentary Portraiture Methodology: Blending Art and Science. *LEARNing Landscapes*, 9(2), 19–27.

Lee, E. (2015). *The making of Asian America: A history*. Simon & Schuster Paperbacks.

Lee, G.-L., & Manning, M. L. (2001). Working with Asian Parents and Families. *Promising Practices*, 9(1), 23–25.

Lee, J. (2022, October 11). How We Rise: Are Asian Americans people of color or the next in line to become white? [web log]. Retrieved May 12, 2023, from https://www.brookings.edu/blog/how-we-rise/2022/10/11/are-asian-americans-people-of-color-or-the-next-in-line-to-become-white/.

Lee, J., & Ramakrishnan, K. (2022, March 16). A Year After Atlanta: As we honor the victims, we ask: how much has anti-Asian hate changed? AAPIData.com. http://aapidata.com/blog/year-after-atlanta/

Lee, S. S. (2006). Over-Represented and De-Minoritized: The Racialization of Asian Americans in Higher Education. *Interactions: UCLA Journal of Education and Information Studies*, 2(2), 1–16.

Loo, T. (2018, December 11). Asian-Settlers Colonialism: Being Chinese in Hawaii. *Honolulu Civil Beat*. https://www.civilbeat.org/2018/12/asian-settlers-colonialism-being-chinese-in-hawaii/#:~:text=Asian%2Dsettler%20colonialism%20is%20when,modern%20cultural%20and%20political%20power

Luo, C. J. (2022, March 16). Perspective | anti-Asian violence is a serious problem. but policing isn't the solution. *The Washington*

Post. https://www.washingtonpost.com/outlook/2022/03/16/anti-asian-violence-is-serious-problem-policing-isnt-solution/

Menjívar, C., & Kanstroom, D. (Eds.). (2013). *Constructing immigrant "illegality": Critiques, experiences, and response*. Cambridge University Press.

Ming Fang He, Bic Ngo, Michelle Bae-Dimitriadis, Cheryl E. Matias, Suniti Sharma, Luis Urrieta Jr & Sophia Rodriguez (2021) Educating Hope, Radicalizing Imagination, and Politicizing Possibility in Hard Times, *Educational Studies*, 57:3, 203–210, DOI: 10.1080/00131946.2021.1893067

Mohanpuhr, A. (2021, March 30). Experts say Atlanta shooting reflects the fetishization of Asian women. *The Stanford Daily*. https://stanforddaily.com/2021/03/29/experts-say-atlanta-shooting-reflects-the-fetishization-of-asian-women/

Molina, N., Hosang, D. M., & Gutiérrez, R. A. (Eds.). *Relational formations of race: Theory, method, and practice* (pp. 257–277). University of California College Press.

Moore, L. (2020, June 26). Universal negro improvement Assn. (UNIA): Encyclopedia of Cleveland history: Case western reserve universityL. Encyclopedia of Cleveland History | Case Western Reserve University.

Museus, S. D., Maramba, D., & Teranishi, R. (Eds.). *The misrepresented minority: New insights on Asian American and Pacific Islanders, and their implications for higher education* (pp. 198–212). Stylus Publishing.

National Center for Education Statistics. (2022). Racial/Ethnic Enrollment in Public Schools. Condition of Education. U.S. Department of Education, Institute of Education Sciences. Retrieved May 11, 2023, from https://nces.ed.gov/programs/coe/indicator/cge.

Ngai, M. (2004). *Impossible subjects: Illegal aliens and the modern making of America*. Princeton University Press.

Ngai, M. (2021, April 21). Racism has always been part of the Asian American experience. *The Atlantic*. Retrieved May 11, 2023, from https://www.theatlantic.com/ideas/archive/2021/04/we-are-constantly-reproducing-anti-asian-racism/618647/.

Okihiro, G. (1994). *Margins and mainstreams: Asians in American history and culture*. University of Washington Press.

Ortiz, N. (2022, February 1). Crip Ecologies: Complicate the Conversation to Reclaim Power. Poetry Foundation. https://www.poetryfoundation.org/poetrymagazine/articles/157104/crip-ecologies-complicate-the-conversation-to-reclaim-power#:~:text=Crip%20ecologies%20describe%20the%20messy,which%20exist%20for%20disabled%20people.

Perea, J. F. (1997). The Black/White Binary Paradigm of Race: The "Normal Science" of American Racial Thought. *California Law Review*, 85(5), 1213–1258. https://doi.org/10.2307/3481059

Park, L. S. H. (2008). Continuing significance of the model minority myth: The second generation. *Social Justice*, 35(2), 134-144.

Paulson, M. (2017, March 17). The battle of "Miss Saigon": Yellowface, art and opportunity. *The New York Times*. https://www.nytimes.com/2017/03/17/theater/the-battle-of-miss-saigon-yellowface-art-and-opportunity.html

Perencevich, E. (2019, December 19). Not all Asians look the same. The Little Hawk. https://www.thelittlehawk.com/52669/opinion/not-all-asians-look-the-same/

Pew Research Center. (2012, June 19). The Rise of Asian Americans Chapter 5: Family and personal values. Pew Research Center's Social & Demographic Trends Project. https://www.pewresearch.org/social-trends/2012/06/19/chapter-5-family-and-personal-values/

Quashie, K. (2021). Black Aliveness, or A Poetics of Being. Duke University Press. https://doi.org/10.2307/j.ctv1dgmm58

Rosalsky, G. (2021, April 20). When you add more police to a city, what happens? NPR. https://www.npr.org/sections/money/2021/04/20/988769793/when-you-add-more-police-to-a-city-what-happens

ross, k.m., (2020). It's time to abolish schools. *Northwestern Magazine*. https://magazine.northwestern.edu/voices/its-time-to-abolish-schools/

Salinas Velasco, C. F., Mazumder, T., & Enriquez, L. E. (2015). "It's not just a Latino issue": Policy recommendations to better support a racially diverse population of undocumented students. *InterActions: UCLA Journal of Education and Information Studies*, 11(1), 1–11.

Santos, A. F., & Hofmann, C. T. (1998, May 4). Prostitution and the bases: A continuing saga of Exploitation. Wordpress. https://catwap.wordpress.com/resources/speeches-papers/prostitution-and-the-bases-a-continuing-saga-of-exploitation/

Sauer, J. S. (2012). Look at Me: Portraiture and Agency. *Disability Studies Quarterly, 32*(4). https://dsq-sds.org/article/view/1736/3180

Schoenbaum, H. (2023, March 23). Transgender youth: "forced outing" bills make schools unsafe. AP NEWS. https://apnews.com/article/transgender-students-pronouns-names-ec0b2c5de329d82c563ffb95262935f3

Shirrell, M., Bristol, T. J., & Britton, T. A. (n.d.). The Effects of Student-Teacher Ethnoracial Matching on Exclusionary Discipline for Asian American, Black, and Latinx Students: Evidence From New York City. https://edworkingpapers.com/sites/default/files/ai21-475.pdf

Smithsonian Asian Pacific American Center. (n.d.). Beyond Bollywood - Indian Americans Shape the Nation. Google. https://artsandculture.google.com/story/jwXRxW5esAsA8A

Smithsonian. (2020, April 24). Black is beautiful: The emergence of Black Culture and identity in the 60s and 70s. National Museum of African American History and Culture. https://nmaahc.si.edu/explore/stories/black-beautiful-emergence-black-culture-and-identity-60s-and-70s#:~:text=In%20its%20philosophy%2C%20%E2%80%9CBlack%20is,in%20the%20African%20American%20community

Superville, D. R. (2023, March 10). Why aren't there more Asian American School Leaders? here's what we heard. Education Week. https://www.edweek.org/leadership/why-arent-there-more-asian-american-school-leaders-heres-what-we-heard/2023/02#:~:text=Less%20than%202%20percent%20of,teaching%20workforce%20in%20public%20schools

Swidler, A. (1986). Culture in Action: Symbols and Strategies. *American Sociological Review, 51*(2), 273–286. https://doi.org/10.2307/2095521

The Asian American Foundation. (2023). STAATUS index 2023: Attitudes towards Asian Americans and Pacific Islanders. staatus-index.s3.amazonaws.com. https://www.taaf.org/project/staatus-index-2023

Tintiangco-Cubales, A (2020). Pinayista - Tatlong Bagsak: Combating Anti-Blackness in the Filipinx Community. YouTube. Retrieved April 26, 2023, from https://www.youtube.com/watch?v=lcTCcTStECk.

Teach for America. (n.d.). Asian American & Pacific Islander Alliances. Teach For America. https://www.teachforamerica. org/asian-american-pacific-islander-alliances

The Sikh Coalition. (n.d.). Fact Sheet on Post-9/11 Discrimination and Violence against Sikh Americans. New York. University of Colorado Boulder. (2020, January). What is community-engaged scholarship? Office for Outreach and Engagement. https://www. colorado.edu/outreach/ooe/community-engaged-scholarship/ what-community-engaged-scholarship

Vargas, J. A. (2018). *Dear America: Notes of an undocumented citizen.* HarperCollins.

Vazquez, T. (n.d.). The Fight for Ethnic Studies. Learning for Justice. Retrieved April 23, 2023, from https://www.learningforjustice. org/magazine/spring-2021/the-fight-for-ethnic-studies

Wang, J. J., Redford, L., & Ratliff, K. A. (2021). Do special education recommendations differ for Asian American and White American students? *Social Psychology of Education*, 24(4), 1065–1083. https://doi.org/10.1007/s11218-021-09645-8

Wikimedia Foundation. (2023, April 20). Military history of Asian Americans. Wikipedia. https://en.wikipedia.org/wiki/ Military_history_of_Asian_Americans

Wu, F. H. (2002). *Yellow: Race in America beyond Black and White.* Basic Books.

Yam, K. (2023, January 11). Why Michelle Yeoh's "Shut up" at the Golden Globes was profound for Asian women. NBCNews.com. https://www.nbcnews.com/news/asian-america/michelle-yeohs-shut-golden-globes-was-profound-asian-women-rcna65365

Yamamoto, E. K. (1997). Critical Race Praxis: Race Theory and Political Lawyering Practice in Post-Civil Rights America. *Michigan Law Review*, 95(4), 821–900. https://doi.org/10.2307/ 1290048

Zavala, M. (2016). Decolonial Methodologies in Education. In: Peters, M. (eds.) *Encyclopedia of Educational Philosophy and Theory.* Springer, Singapore. https://doi.org/10.1007/ 978-981-287-532-7_498-1

Index

Page numbers followed by *f* refer to figures.